The Student Cookbook

Ingredients • Techniques • Recipes

The Cookbook Library

Flame Tree has been creating **family-friendly**, **classic** and **beginner recipes** for our best-selling cookbooks for over ten years now. Our mission is to offer you a wide range of **expert-tested** dishes, while providing **straightforward** step-by-step photos and clear images of the final dish so that you can match it to your own results. Further information is available at **FlameTreeRecipes.com**

Publisher & Creative Director: Nick Wells
Senior Project Editor: Catherine Taylor
Art Director: Mike Spender
Digital Design & Production: Chris Herbert
Production Controller: Digby Smith
Proofreader: Eileen Cox

Special thanks to Alex McClean (Introduction), Gina Steer for her continued help and contributions and Laura Bulbeck.

This is a **FLAME TREE** Book

FLAME TREE PUBLISHING
Crabtree Hall, Crabtree Lane
Fulham, London SW6 6TY
United Kingdom
www.flametreepublishing.com

Flame Tree is part of Flame Tree Publishing Ltd

First published 2012

Copyright © 2012 Flame Tree Publishing Ltd

12 14 16 15 13
3 5 7 9 10 12 11 8 6 4

ISBN: 978-0-85775-383-0

Printed in Singapore

Publisher's Note: Raw or semi-cooked eggs should not be consumed by babies, toddlers, pregnant or breast-feeding women, the elderly or those suffering from a recurring illness.

A copy of the CIP data for this book is available from the British Library.

All images © The Foundry Creative Media Co. Ltd, except: Courtesy of Shutterstock.com and © the following photographers: 14 mangostock; 15 CandyBox Images; 17l Ingrid Balabanova; 17r Matt Grant; 18 Kacso Sandor; 19 Elena Elisseeva; 20 Elen; 22 ifong; 26 Olga Drabovich; 27 Steve Cukrov; 28 My Lit'l Eye; 29 Mirabelle Pictures; 30 Julian Rovagnati; 31 ventdusud; 32, 33, 55l Viktor1; 34 Nicholas Rjabow; 35 M. Unal Ozmen; 36 Robert Anthony; 38 Anthony Berenyi; 39 Piotr Rzeszutek; 40 Cogipix; 42 Allen W Yoo; 43 cenap refik ongan; 44l Robyn Mackenzie; 44r Péter Gudella; 45 fredredhat; 46 James Peragine; 47, 50 Joe Gough; 48 Photoseeker; 49 Steven Collins; 51 Douglas Freer; 52 Brett Mulcahy; 53l Monika Wisniewska; 53r Jaimie Duplass; 54 bogumil; 55r badahos; 56 Christopher Elwell; 57 D7INAMI7S; 58 Olga Miltsova; 60 kajakiki.

The Student Cookbook

Ingredients • Techniques • Recipes

General Editor: Gina Steer

**FLAME TREE
PUBLISHING**

Contents

The first part of this book is intended to set you up. From handy **conversions** and reminders about **nutrition**, to the essential **tools and equipment** that you'll need along with key **store-cupboard ingredients**. It also covers **basic cooking methods** for things like **eggs**, **rice**, **pasta and potatoes** and info on **meat and veg**. Give it a good read if you can, before jumping into the tasty recipe sections that follow.

Soups 62

Soup is probably one of the **simplest** things to make as a student – no really! It can be **healthy** and **hearty** and you can chuck in anything that you like, and they **store well** too. Most soups can be mashed to the desired consistency by hand, but you might find a cheap handheld blender a godsend – especially if you like your soups smooth. Here is a great selection to inspire you.

Smaller Meals & Sides 92

As a young, energetic student, you probably require your dinner to be pretty filling. However, occasionally you may want something a little lighter for **lunch** or as a **snack** or as a **side dish** when you cook for friends. Well, here is a selection of dishes that won't leave you hungry, but still leave a little room for those cheesy chips you know you're going to succumb to at the union later.

Easy-Peasy Pasta 128

What would we do without pasta? It is **cheap** to buy and **lasts for ages** in the store cupboard; it is **quick** to cook and so **versatile**; it goes with pretty much anything. In this delicious selection we have some **classics** and some more **adventurous** dishes, from bakes to spaghetti, from rich cheesy sauces to spicy tomato. Some make enough to freeze for when you want an easy dinner to reheat.

Essential Curries 152

Curry is a **fave student nosh**. But don't forget that you can make all manner of delicious curries yourself **quickly and easily** – there's no need for loads of greasy and expensive takeaways. Here we provide a diverse selection, from variations on the classics, **balti** and **korma**, to Thai and Caribbean-style curries. And there are lots of **veggie** choices too.

Rice & Noodles..........184

Pasta and potatoes are all well and good but it can get boring, so **vary your carb** intake along with your **flavours** with some delish rice and noodle dishes. Here we include some **classic sweet-and-sour, chow mein** and **Thai** dishes, alongside some **interesting** rice nuggets and a comforting Sausage & Bacon Risotto. Mmmm!

Veggie Treats 210

You will soon discover, if you didn't know already, that vegetables are much **cheaper than meat** – as well as **healthier** and **safer** to cook! If you are someone who expects meat with every main meal, then think again – this selection of recipes will help you discover that veg really can be the **star of the show**: from lighter Rice-filled Peppers to hearty casseroles and burgers.

Hearty Meals..244

Sometimes you just want something you can tuck into, something that will **fill your belly** and warm your cockles. Well, here we've got a tempting array of hearty, **traditional** fare and some slightly **more original dishes**. We show you how to make the best-ever sausage and mash and a wonderfully comforting Shepherd's Pie. If you're feeling more **cosmopolitan**, how about Creamy Chicken Stroganoff or Cassoulet?

Impress your Friends............................268

You won't always be cooking for one – with your newfound cooking skills it's inevitable that **friends** will be clamouring to be fed by you, and you might even manage some sophisticated '**dinner parties**'. Not to mention – it would be great to surprise your **parents** when they come to visit. Here are a few suggestions of meals that you can make for **groups**, which you may not otherwise have the chance to make, since they **don't store so well**, may take a little longer to prepare or are a bit more of a drain on the wallet.

Treats & Desserts...........288

Now I know that you're probably thinking, 'I'll be impressed if I can cook a decent dinner every night – I'm never going to get round to baking', but once you realize how easy it is to whip up savoury meals, and that you can save leftovers for instant food, you may want to **try your hand** at some of these treats. For example, you can't exactly afford a fantastic present, so how great would it be to make cake for a friend's **birthday**? Cookies are quick and easy and will be a **huge hit with your mates**, and Chocolate & Fruit Crumble is a **fab and easy dessert**.

Introduction

Most students go off to university feeling confident, grown up and completely sure of their own ability to look after themselves. Of course, then they get there and realise that not only do they have to make new friends, find their way around a new place and study what is possibly a new subject at a much higher level, but Mum and Dad aren't there to do the washing and make the dinner. This book won't remind you to put your washing on, or stop you from putting that one red sock in making all of your whites pink, but it will help make the daunting prospect of cooking simple and possibly even enjoyable.

Money, Money, Money

First things first: food is expensive. That's just one of those sad facts of life we all have to get used to...but that doesn't mean you have to live off baked beans for the next three years. You can if you want to but it's unlikely you would have picked up this book if you intended to do that. It's possible to eat decent food while staying within your student budget and leaving enough money to go out for drinks. It's all about what you cook, how you cook it and how you store it. The recipes you'll find in here give guidelines for how to get the most out of what freezer space you have, show you how to cook anything from a boiled egg to risotto (actually risotto is easy, but looks really impressive if you cook it for a date, or friends), all within a budget. Some recipes can be made a bit fancier if you're cooking right after you get your loan, or cheaper if it's those last few weeks before the next instalment.

Get Kitted Out and Stock Up

It would be useful before you do your first food shop (don't worry if it's too late, you can nip to the local supermarket and pick up anything you need) to have a read through the first part of this book. That will let you know what you're likely to need and what's useful to have in your cupboard for those days you overran at the library, or had every intention of going to the library and went to the pub, and you don't have long before you go out. Don't forget about equipment either – you don't need anything fancy, but there are some things that are worth spending a few quid on that will come in handy again and again.

The Basics

You'll also see useful information such as how to cook eggs or potatoes and a quick guide to what all those cooking words mean. If you already know all of that, then great, smile smugly to yourself and only refer to that bit if you forget. Everyone else, have a good look and save yourself the embarrassment of needing to call home every night to ask.

Get Cooking

The recipes themselves are pretty easy to do, and lots of them will do more than one meal so you won't waste all the food that only comes in packs of twos or more. Even the more complicated-looking

recipes are easier than you think. Eating food you have made instead of takeaway every night saves you a fortune and helps stave off the dreaded Freshers' Flu, not to mention makes you feel pretty good about yourself. So ditch the beans and the pizza menu, grab that wooden spoon and have a go.

Useful Conversions

Liquid Measures

Metric	Imperial
2.5 ml	½ teaspoon
5 ml	1 teaspoon
15 ml	1 tablespoon
25 ml	1 fl oz
50 ml	2 fl oz
65 ml	2½ fl oz
85 ml	3 fl oz
100 ml	3½ fl oz
125 ml	4 fl oz
135 ml	4½ fl oz
150 ml	¼ pint (5 fl oz)
175 ml	6 fl oz
200 ml	7 fl oz (⅓ pint)
250 ml	8 fl oz
275 ml	9 fl oz
300 ml	½ pint (10 fl oz)
350 ml	12 fl oz
400 ml	14 fl oz
450 ml	¾ pint (15 fl oz)
475 ml	16 fl oz
500 ml	18 fl oz
600 ml	1 pint (20 fl oz)
750 ml	1¼ pints
900 ml	1½ pints
1 litre	1¾ pints
1.1 litres	2 pints
1.25 litres	2¼ pints
1.5 litres	2½ pints
1.6 litres	2¾ pints
1.7 litres	3 pints
2 litres	3½ pints
2.25 litres	4 pints
2.5 litres	4½ pints
2.75 litres	5 pints

Temperature Conversion

°F	°C		°F	°C
−4°F	−20°C		68°F	20°C
5°F	−15°C		77°F	25°C
14°F	−10°C		86°F	30°C
23°F	−5°C		95°F	35°C
32°F	0°C		104°F	40°C
41°F	5°C		113°F	45°C
50°F	10°C		122°F	50°C
59°F	15°C		212°F	100°C

Dry Weights

Metric	Imperial	Metric	Imperial
10 g	¼ oz	350 g	12 oz
15 g	½ oz	375 g	13 oz
20 g	¾ oz	400 g	14 oz
25 g	1 oz	425 g	15 oz
40 g	1½ oz	450 g	1 lb (16 oz)
50 g	2 oz		
65 g	2½ oz		
75 g	3 oz		
100 g	3½ oz		
125 g	4 oz		
130 g	4½ oz		
150 g	5 oz		
165 g	5½ oz		
175 g	6 oz		
185 g	6½ oz		
200 g	7 oz		
225 g	8 oz		
250 g	9 oz		
275 g	10 oz		
300 g	11 oz		
325 g	11½ oz		

Oven Temperatures

110°C	225°F	Gas Mark ¼	Very slow oven
120/130°C	250°F	Gas Mark ½	Very slow oven
140°C	275°F	Gas Mark 1	Slow oven
150°C	300°F	Gas Mark 2	Slow oven
160/170°C	325°F	Gas Mark 3	Moderate oven
180°C	350°F	Gas Mark 4	Moderate oven
190°C	375°F	Gas Mark 5	Moderately hot
200°C	400°F	Gas Mark 6	Moderately hot
220°C	425°F	Gas Mark 7	Hot oven
230°C	450°F	Gas Mark 8	Hot oven
240°C	475°F	Gas Mark 9	Very hot oven

Good Cooking Rules

When handling and cooking foods, there are a few rules and guidelines that should be observed so that food remains fit to eat and uncontaminated with the bacteria and bugs that can result in food poisoning.

Good Hygiene Rules

- Personal hygiene is imperative when handling food. Before commencing, wash hands thoroughly with soap, taking particular care with

nails. Always wash hands after going to the toilet. Wash again after handling raw foods, cooked meats or vegetables. Do not touch any part of the body or handle pets, rubbish or dirty washing during food preparation.
- Cuts should be covered with a waterproof plaster, preferably blue so it can be easily seen if lost.
- Keep all surfaces clean using antibacterial cleanser and clean cloths.
- Ensure that hair is off the face and does not trail into food or machinery.
- Use a dishwasher wherever possible and wash utensils and equipment in very hot, soapy water.
- Use clean dish cloths and tea towels, replacing regularly or boiling them to kill any bacteria.
- Chopping boards and cooking implements must be clean. Boards should either be washed in a dishwasher or scrubbed after each use. Keep a separate board for meat, fish and vegetables and wash knives before using on different types of food. Use separate boards for raw and cooked food or wash them thoroughly in-between.
- Use dustbin liners for rubbish and empty regularly, cleaning your bin with disinfectant. Dustbins should be outside.

Guidelines for Using a Refrigerator

- Ensure that the refrigerator is situated away from any equipment that gives off heat, such as the cooker, washing machine or tumble drier, to ensure the greatest efficiency. Ensure that the vents are not obstructed.
- If not frost-free, defrost regularly, wiping down with a mild solution of bicarbonate of soda dissolved in warm water and a clean cloth.
- Close the door as quickly as possible so that the motor does not have to work overtime to keep it at the correct temperature.
- Ensure that the temperature is 5°C. A thermometer is a good investment.
- Avoid over-loading – this just makes the motor work harder.
- Cool food before placing in the refrigerator and always cover to avoid any smells or transference of taste to other foods.
- Remove supermarket packaging from raw meat, poultry and fish, place on a plate or dish, cover loosely and store at the base of the refrigerator to ensure that the juices do not drip on other foods.
- Store cheese in a box or container, wrapped to prevent the cheese drying out.
- Remove food to be eaten raw 30 minutes before use so it can return to room temperature.

- Cooked meats, bacon and all cooked dishes should be stored at the top – this is the coldest part.
- Store eggs in the egg compartment and remove 30 minutes before cooking in order to return them to temperature.
- Butter and all fats can be stored on the door, as can milk, cold drinks, sauces, mayonnaise and preserves with low sugar content.
- Cream and other dairy products, as well as pastries such as chocolate éclairs, should be stored on the middle shelf.
- Vegetables, salad and fruit should be stored in the salad boxes at the bottom of the refrigerator.
- Soft fruits should be kept in the salad box along with mushrooms, which are best kept in paper bags.

- To avoid cross-contamination, raw and cooked foods must be stored separately.
- Use all foods by the sell-by date – once opened, treat as cooked foods and use within two days.

Freezing Rules and Tips

- When buying frozen foods, transport in freezer-insulated bags, placing in the freezer as soon as possible after purchase.
- Do not re-freeze any thawed frozen foods unless cooked first.
- Date and label frozen food and use in rotation.
- Ensure that all food is thoroughly thawed before use, unless meant to be cooked from frozen.
- Freezer bags can be better for smaller spaces, as they allow you to use less space in your freezer than solid containers.
- Do not attempt to home freeze any large joints or chickens. This is because the domestic freezer does not reach a low enough temperature fast enough and in the time taken to freeze, toxins may start to grow.

Open Freezing

Some food, such as individual portions of fish, meat or cake, benefit from being frozen individually rather than all being put into a bag to freeze. This is called open freezing. Simply put the items to be frozen on a tray lined with nonstick baking paper, ensuring that they do not touch each other. Place in the freezer and freeze until completely frozen. Pack into a freezer bag or container, label and date before returning to the freezer as quickly as possible. When wishing to defrost a portion, remove from the bag or container and place on a plate and allow to thaw. Do not add other food to the original frozen food at a later date.

Freezing Rice

It is possible to freeze rice but many experts strongly advise home cooks against it. This is because rice contains spores that are harmful and cannot be killed by reheating. If still wishing to freeze rice, the best method is to cool the rice very quickly after cooking. Place a thin layer on a tray and cover to help cool the rice. Once cool, place portions into freezer bags and freeze. When wishing to use, thaw, then reheat to at least 75°C for 2 minutes, then eat. Do not freeze again.

Defrosting Freezers

It is important that the freezer is allowed to defrost at least every 6 months and the cabinet is cleaned both inside and out. This ensures that there are no little packages lurking at the back or bottom of the freezer and the risk of passing toxins onto fresh frozen food is kept to a minimum. Use old towels and trays to mop up and collect the water, emptying the trays regularly. Clean the inside of the cabinet and any drawers or trays with a solution of bicarbonate of soda and warm water. Use 1 tablespoon of bicarbonate of soda to 1.1 litres/2 pints warm water. Dry with a clean cloth and allow to reach the correct temperature before placing any food in the freezer.

General Rules

- Use all foods by the use-by date and store correctly. This applies to all foods: fresh, frozen, canned and dried. Potatoes are best if removed from polythene, stored in brown paper and kept in the cool and dark.
- Cook all poultry thoroughly at the correct temperature (190°C/375°F/Gas Mark 5) ensuring that the juices run clear.
- Leave foods to cool as quickly as possible before placing in the refrigerator, and cover while cooling.
- Reheat foods thoroughly until piping hot. Remember to allow foods to stand when using the microwave and stir to distribute the heat.
- Microwaves vary according to make and wattage – always refer to manufacturer's instructions.
- Only reheat dishes once and always heat until piping hot.
- Ensure that eggs are fresh. If using for mayonnaise, soufflés or other dishes that use raw or semi-cooked egg, do not give to the vulnerable – the elderly, pregnant women, those with a recurring illness, toddlers and babies.
- Chilled foods, such as cold meats, cheese, fresh meat, fish and dairy products should be bought, taken home and placed in the refrigerator immediately. Do not keep in a warm car or room.
- Avoid buying damaged or unlabelled canned goods. Keep store cupboards clean, wiping down regularly and rotating the food.
- Flour, nuts, rice, pulses, grains and pasta should be checked regularly and, once opened, placed in airtight containers.
- Do not buy eggs or frozen or chilled foods that are damaged in any way.
- Keep dried herbs and ready-ground spices in a cool, dark place. They quickly lose their pungency and flavour when exposed to light.

Nutrition

Good nutrition is essential at any time – especially when you may be still growing and need to keep up with the rigours of study and socialising. Our bodies need a variety of different foods in order for them to work properly and for us to remain healthy. Food on a budget does not mean that nutritious food and well-balanced meals are off the agenda. Food should have flavour and look great, but it should be good for us too.

What are Nutrients?

These are chemical compounds that are present in food. They supply energy for the body and help build and replace cells. They also help to regulate our bodies' processes. Not including water, there are five categories of nutrients: carbohydrates, fats, proteins, vitamins and minerals. To this list you could also add 'fibre'. This is not really a nutrient as such, but is nevertheless very necessary for a healthy, functioning body.

What About Calories?

A calorie (written as 'kcal' on food labels) is just a measurement of energy. It is actually defined as the amount of heat needed to raise the temperature of 1 kg of water by 1°C. We need this energy, but there is enormous debate about how many calories adult humans need to eat every day in order to remain healthy. Broadly, men need around 2,700 calories a day and women about 2,000. Up to 60 per cent of those calories can come from carbohydrates, 20 per cent from proteins and up to 20 per cent from fats.

Calorie Content in Carbohydrate, Protein and Fat

Without sufficient food energy a body cannot function properly. So how many calories can the three basic nutritional elements give you?

Carbohydrate 1 oz (28 g) of carbohydrate contains 112 calories.

Protein The same amount of protein contains 112 calories.

Fat The same amount of fat contains 252 calories.

Food from animals tends to be higher in fat, and some products, such as fruit, vegetables and grains are naturally low in fat. But beware, because some grocery items like French fries or croissants are prepared with fat.

Carbohydrates

These are an important source of food energy. Carbohydrates exist in two forms: complex and simple. Complex carbohydrates, which contain starches and fibre, are the best as they provide a slower-burning and thus more constant supply of energy. Complex carbohydrates that contain refined starches are not so good for you, however. Simple carbohydrates are sugars. Some are natural whilst others are refined – again, the refined kind are particularly bad for you. Examples of foods that contain carbohydrates are:

Complex carbohydrates (starches) Brown rice; wholemeal breads, grains, cereals, flour and pasta; beans and peas; root vegetables; bananas.

Complex carbohydrates (refined starches) White bread, flour, pasta and rice; processed breakfast cereals; pizzas; biscuits, pastries and cakes.

Simple carbohydrates (sugars) The natural ones are in fruit and vegetables. Even these can cause tooth decay.

Simple carbohydrates (refined sugars) Chocolate; honey; jams; soft drinks; sweets and snacks; prepared food and sauces; biscuits, cakes and pastries.

Fibre

Fibre is basically carbohydrate that the body cannot use, so it does not supply the body with energy. However, it is essential in helping the intestinal tract to work properly and flush out waste. Dietary fibre can also prevent some kinds of cancer. It can be found in whole grains and fruit and vegetables, provided they are eaten raw.

Fats

Cholesterol (an element of animal fat) is often portrayed as the developed world's health time bomb. It is linked to heart disease and it is found in a wide variety of food, such as beef, pork, poultry, butter, egg yolks, liver, shellfish and dairy products. However, cholesterol is an important part of a healthy body and it is only when it reaches high levels in the blood that it becomes a danger. In fact, fat in general is a very necessary element of the diet, but some are better than others:

Saturated fats These are fats that are solid at room temperature. You find them in dairy products, animal fats, fatty meat, some oils and foods such as chocolate. These are the ones that contribute to health problems.

Polyunsaturated fats Found in fish and soybean, and sunflower, corn and safflower oils. They are considered to be more healthy options.

Monounsaturated fats These can be found in olive oil and whole grains and nuts. These too are considered to be more healthy.

Trans fats These are types of unsaturated fat that can be polyunsaturated or monounsaturated, but which have become more like saturated fat, usually by virtue of a process of partial hydrogenation. Trans fats have been linked to an elevated risk of coronary heart disease, so it is advisable to avoid foods (typically processed foods) which contain partially hydrogenated vegetable oils.

Proteins

Proteins are amino acids necessary for all sorts of complicated functions within our cells. The body can make its own amino acids, but there are eight types that it can't make so we need to get them from food. This is why we need to have dairy products, poultry, fish, eggs and meat in our diet. You can get all the amino acids you need if you eat beans and rice together, or if you combine cornmeal bread and chilli beans. Proteins are essential for building body tissue and the body can also use them for energy.

Vitamins and Minerals

Both of these are essential but neither contains energy. Key vitamins and minerals, and examples of what foods contain them are as follows:

Vitamin A Contained in mango, broccoli, squashes, carrots and pumpkins.

Vitamin B Contained in spinach, peas, tomato, water melon and potatoes.

Vitamin C Contained in spinach, peppers, kiwi fruit, strawberries and citrus fruits.

Vitamin D Contained in egg yolks, liver and oily fish.

Vitamin E Contained in wheat germ, avocado, sweet potatoes and tofu.

Vitamin K Contained in leafy green vegetables, broccoli, cabbage and liver.

Calcium A mineral contained in milk, cheese and sardines.

Iron A mineral contained in artichokes, spinach and clams.

Iodine A mineral contained in salt, seafood, bread and milk.

Sodium The easiest way to take in the mineral sodium is through salt, but not too much because it causes high blood pressure. It is also in soy sauce, bread and milk.

Potassium A mineral contained in potatoes, green beans and bananas.

The Balanced Diet

You don't need to know the science behind nutrition, or to make things complicated for yourself. Simply aim for a truly balanced diet and your body should receive everything it needs. The plate concept shown on page 22 gives an idea of the kind of proportions in which you should eat the different food groups, but mainly just follow some golden rules:

Variety: Eat a variety of foods to provide your body with everything it needs. 'Eat a rainbow a day to keep the doctor away.'

Exercise: Balance your food with physical activity, to improve fitness and help your body make the most of its healthy diet.

Natural and wholesome: Eat plenty of whole grains, vegetables and fruit.

Keep a check on fats: Avoid saturated fats to keep your cholesterol down.

Keep a check on sugars: Don't include too many sugars in your diet.

Keep a check on salt: Reduce the amount of salt and sodium to avoid high blood pressure – adults should consume no more than 6 g a day. Remember that high salt quantities may be hiding in processed foods.

Drink alcohol in moderation: It supplies calories but little or no nutrients. I know this is a difficult one!

Tools & Equipment

In this section, I have listed the tools and equipment you will need in order to start cooking, Some of the tools and equipment are absolutely essential and I would recommend that you invest in these first. Other less-essential tools and equipment can also be reasonably expensive, so they might be good ideas to suggest as either birthday or Christmas presents.

Essential Tools

Knives Knives are perhaps the most important tools in the kitchen. It is advisable to have a good selection. First, when buying, make sure that any knife sits comfortably in your hand. You will need a small knife (often called a 'paring' knife) for all the little jobs, such as deseeding a chilli and cutting fruits and vegetables into small pieces. At least a further three to four additional knives would be good: a large chef's knife, which has a long wide blade, is ideal for chopping both meat and fish as well as fresh herbs; a carving knife; a bread knife, with or without a serrated edge; and a medium-sized all-purpose knife for all other jobs. Make sure that the knives are a reputable brand and easy to sharpen – a good knife will last a long while, maybe for ever.

Wooden Spoons I feel you can never have too many wooden spoons! Although they will not last for ever, looked after and washed properly they should last for at least one to two years, depending on what you use them for. I would recommend buying one of the sets that are so readily available. These normally come in different lengths – the shorter one is super for sauces and the other two for stirring food, such as meat that is being sealed in a pan, as well as for mixing cakes and batters. Although they wash perfectly well, it is a good idea to keep some spoons for sweet dishes and others for savoury dishes. Then there are the wooden spatulas which are perfect for omelettes or frying meats such as chops, as the flat, wider area makes turning food over so much easier.

Large Spoons These can be a plain spoon, ideal for stirring or dishing out casseroles, stews and vegetables, or a slotted draining spoon – this refers to the gaps in the bowl of the spoon which allow any liquid to drain out, back into the pan, for example, when removing meat after sealing it for a stew or casserole.

Measuring Spoons These ensure that the correct amount of an ingredient is used (such as $1/4$ teaspoon or 1 tablespoon). This is especially useful when either following a specific diet (for example, where oil and butter intake needs to be measured), or for use with a thickening agent such as cornflour, or with spices, where too much could completely ruin the dish.

Spatula Also known as a 'fish slice', this is not the more ornate, usually silver utensil, used when

serving fish in front of guests, but the plastic or metal utensil with slotted holes that is superb for turning food over and for removing cooked food from hot baking trays or roasting tins – plastic is kinder on nonstick pans but may not be as durable. They also come in wooden versions, which are normally narrower with a slightly slanted or flat base.

Vegetable Peeler Using a peeler makes the job easier and will ensure that you get an even look to the peeled fruit or vegetable, such as peeling pears for cooking in wine or peeling potatoes. I prefer the swivel-blade peeler as it only removes a very thin layer and this will mean that, since many of the nutrients are just below the skin, they are preserved. However, it is a matter of personal choice, so when buying, try imitating the peeling action and see which fits you most comfortably.

Grater For grating cheese, carrots and other root vegetables, fresh root ginger, chocolate, citrus zest and nutmeg – those last two should be done on the finest side of the grater.

Extra Tools

Ladle Perfect for hot soups, casseroles, stews and any other hot liquids that need transferring or serving.

Potato Masher You would be quite stuck without this if you wanted to make mashed potatoes, and it is handy for chunky soups too. It is superb for mashing all manner of vegetables, from potatoes to parsnips, carrots, yams or sweet potatoes.

Kebab Sticks and Skewers Not essential at all – unless you want to make kebabs! Either metal or wooden, kebab sticks are for cooking both savoury and sweet kebabs, koftas and satays, and skewering fish or chicken into 'spatchcock' shape – this is where the food is split almost in half, then skewered to keep its shape prior to cooking. Remember that wooden kebab sticks need soaking in cold water for at least 30 minutes and both ends wrapped in kitchen foil to prevent the ends from burning and the cook burning her or his fingers. Skewers are similar to kebab sticks but are always made of metal. They can be used for kebabs but are also perfect for testing whether cakes are cooked in the middle, or if poultry is completely cooked – especially when cooking turkeys, as the very long skewers will go right through the thickest part straight to the centre cavity.

Whisks Used for whisking eggs, whipping cream or sauces in order to create a smooth consistency and incorporate air. They are usually formed from interlocking wires and are available in various types, most commonly the balloon whisk of varying sizes, the mechanically hand-operated rotary whisk and a flat whisk. All work well but take longer than one powered by electricity – *see page 30*.

Basic Equipment

Certain pieces of equipment are essential when cooking. There is no need to go out and spend a fortune, as most of the equipment is relatively cheap. However, what I would recommend is that you buy good quality pans, ones that will not buckle in the heat after being used a couple of times. Nonstick pans can also make life a lot easier when it comes to the washing up. Below is a list of equipment that will start the beginner cook on their way and can easily be added to after a little time and some experience is gained.

Chopping Boards Essential for any job that involves cutting. Look for the colour co-ordinated boards, so that you can use a different colour for different types of food (that is, to keep meat, especially chicken, separate from vegetables, for example). That way, there will be no cross-contamination of food. Make sure that you wash them thoroughly after use, washing in the dishwasher if you have one.

Measuring Jug Essential for measuring liquids, with the measurements marked down the side of the jug. These are available in different sizes and again can be bought as glass Pyrex jugs or in plastic.

Scales These are essential in British cooking, especially when baking. Most scales, whether digital or conventional, measure in both grams and ounces, and all have a bowl in which to place the ingredients to be measured.

Mixing Bowls Ideally, you will have at least three – in small, medium and large. These can be Pyrex glass or similar and are essential for many jobs in the kitchen, including soaking, storing, creaming butter and sugar for cakes, pastry making, melting chocolate, whipping cream and whisking egg whites.

Pans Perhaps the most expensive investment when first beginning to cook. I would recommend that you buy a set of saucepans, as normally there are three to five of differing sizes and these should be adequate to begin with. A good frying pan is important, preferably with a lid to increase its versatility. You might also like to have a milk (small) pan for making sauces as well as boiling milk.

Colander and Sieve Used for sifting flours and straining ingredients to remove any lumps, a sieve is usually made of fine mesh wire, while a colander tends to be rather bigger, with bigger holes or slots, and is used for draining cooked pasta and vegetables. The latter come in plastic and metal versions.

Baking Trays Those without edges all round are often referred to as 'sheets'. Baking trays have many varied uses. Dishes such as lasagne can be placed on baking trays so that they are easy to place in the oven as well as remove. They are also good for baking such items as scones, meringues and cookies as well as using to reheat dishes. Other baking equipment can be bought as it is required; to begin with, I would suggest that you keep it to the minimum with one or two baking trays.

Clingfilm, Food Boxes and Bags You are bound to have leftovers that you do not want to waste, so it is essential that you have clingfilm for covering food to be put in the fridge, a few freezer-safe plastic boxes with securely fitting lids and some plastic freezer bags – as we have said, freezer bags can be better if you're tight on space, as they take up less room in your freezer than solid containers.

Extra Equipment

Handheld Blender Out of the items in this list, this is the cheapest and easiest and thus the first and only one that a student should consider buying. Also known as immersion blenders, they can be bought for less than a tenner in big supermarkets, and do the job well and conveniently – ideal if you plan to make soups.

Blender or Liquidiser Very similar to a food processor, having a jug rather than a bowl. Blends and chops but does not do all the jobs that a food processor will do.

Food Mixer These can be freestanding and perform many jobs in the kitchen from whipping cream, whisking egg whites, creaming butter and sugar for baking cakes to making dough for bread and rubbing in pastry, or simply placing all the ingredients in the bowl and mixing. Smaller, cheaper hand-held versions are available, which you may greatly appreciate if you plan to make more than the odd cake – hand whisking and beating can be tiring after a while!

Food Processor A very versatile piece of equipment and one that I would recommend keen cooks investing in – but perhaps a few years down the line. It will chop vegetables, fruit, nuts and herbs, and shred vegetables, as well as blend soups, make pastry dough and even cakes. Available at different prices.

Terminology

Over the years, the language of cooking has developed and now there are many new words and expressions, which perhaps twenty-five years ago no one would have dreamt of using in connection with cooking. In any case, below are some of the basic words you are likely to come across.

Al dente Used to describe pasta when it is cooked to the desired amount – that is, tender but still firm to the bite. It is important not to overcook pasta.

Baking Cooking foods in the oven. This normally applies primarily to cakes, breads, pastries and puddings, but can refer to anything cooked in the dry heat of the oven. 'Baking' is often used interchangeably with 'roasting', but a distinction can arguably be drawn by saying that 'roasting' implies greater heat and more pronounced browning. 'Roasting' is also the preferred term for meat, poultry and vegetables, while 'baking' tends to be reserved for fish, seafood and the items mentioned above.

Basting Brushing or drizzling meat or fish with its own juices, oil or a prepared sauce, while roasting or grilling, to add flavour and retain moisture.

Beating Using a wooden spoon to mix ingredients together until smooth, such as when making batter for pancakes or Yorkshire pudding.

Blanching Pouring boiling water over fresh green vegetables (or immersing them into boiling water for a short time) in order to preserve the colour. They are then typically plunged into cold water to halt the cooking process. This is done when vegetables are either to be frozen or added to a dish towards the end of cooking. It will also speed up their cooking time.

Bruising Slightly crushing an ingredient, usually with the flat side of a chef's knife or a rolling pin, in order to release its flavour.

Creaming Beating butter or margarine with sugar until lighter in colour and soft and creamy in texture. This applies to cake making.

Drizzling Pouring a little sauce or oil over food while taking care not to swamp it.

Dropping consistency This applies in particular to sponges. The finished unbaked mixture should gently fall off the wooden spoon when it is lightly tapped on the edge of the bowl.

En papillote Food wrapped in paper – usually baking parchment – and cooked in the oven. The dish is normally served still in the paper so that, on opening, the eater gets the full aroma from the spices and flavours used.

Flaking Separating fish into fine flakes.

Folding in This applies to stirring another ingredient into an uncooked mixture such as a meringue or sponge cake mixture. Care must be taken that the mixture is not overmixed, as this will remove the air that has been whisked in, thus preventing a good rise or the required light texture.

Frying Cooking fresh food in, normally, a frying pan or, sometimes, a deep-fat fryer, cooking it to a certain stage or completely. Food is fried in oil or fat until cooked (fats include dripping, lard, margarine, ghee and butter).

Glazing Brushing a food with egg, butter or other liquid, sometimes prior to cooking, to give a good colour or to enhance the finished dish.

Infusing Liquids are heated gently with seasonings or flavours, then left for the flavours to develop in the liquid.

Julienne The style of cut whereby vegetables or zest are cut into very thin strips, often for garnish.

Jus The natural juices from cooking meat, often used as a gravy. The word is also used to mean a slightly more elaborate kind of sauce reduction based on the 'jus'.

Kneading This applies mainly to pastry and bread. The just-made dough is placed on a floured surface. Using the knuckles, the dough is stretched and folded over on itself until smooth. This stretches the dough and makes it more elastic and pliable.

Reduction The process and result of boiling a liquid to both reduce the amount and to make the flavour more intense.

Refreshing Plunging vegetables into cold water to stop the cooking process and to preserve the colour. The vegetables are normally reheated before serving.

Roux A cooked butter and flour paste, normally in equal quantities, used to thicken sauces. Small amounts are added to simmering liquid and whisked in, or the roux is made in a small pan and warm liquid stirred in, then the pan is placed over a gentle heat and cooked, stirring, until thickened.

Sautéing This simply means frying, and refers mainly to the cooking of meat and vegetables in a frying pan when first starting to cook in order to

seal in the meat juices and help preserve their nutrients and flavour.

Scoring Making cuts into pork or gammon rind, both for decorative effect and to help the food cook more quickly.

Searing Cooking meat or other foods very quickly under the grill or in the oven in order to seal in the juices and to give a golden brown appearance.

Sifting Shaking icing sugar or flour through a sieve, to remove any lumps and to aerate in order to help with the rising of cakes.

Simmering When liquid is brought to the boil, then the heat is reduced so that a few bubbles gently break the surface. If the bubbles do not appear, increase the heat slightly.

Steaming A method of cooking food with steam, rather than directly in water. Vegetables are especially good if steamed, as most of the nutrients are preserved and not lost into the water, as happens when they are boiled. Food is placed in a container that will allow the steam to pass through,

which sits on top of a pan with gently simmering water. The steamer is covered with a lid.

Whipping This is when whipping or double cream is beaten with a whisk until soft peaks are formed in the thickened cream. Can be whipped either by machine or by a handheld whisk such as a balloon whisk.

Whisking Beating with a whisk – usually egg whites, either with a food mixer or using a handheld whisk, until the egg white is stiff and dry (this means that the bowl of whisked egg whites can be tipped upside down and the egg white does not move).

Zest What is the difference between 'zest' and 'rind'? 'Zest' is the outermost part of the 'rind' of a citrus fruit, as opposed to the white 'pith' underneath, but in a cooking context can refer to the long thin strips of zest made with a 'zester' (which are used for decoration only, as, if eaten, will give a bitter taste) or to grated zest, which is made by rubbing the unpeeled but washed or scrubbed fruit up and down the fine side of a grater, giving very fine pieces. As these are thinner than zest strips, they can be used to flavour dishes.

Store Cupboard Essentials

The first food shopping trip should be focused on setting up a well-targeted store cupboard. There are lots of ingredients that you can expect to use again and again but which you should not have to buy on a frequent basis.

When thinking about essentials, think of flavour, something that is going to add to a dish without increasing its fat content. It is worth spending a bit more money on these products to make flavoursome dishes that will help stop the urge to snack on fatty foods.

What to Stock in Your Store Cupboard

Store the ingredients in a cool, dark place and remember to rotate them. Most will be safe to use for six months.

Herbs and spices Certain key herbs and spices are essential for flavoursome food. Often it is preferable to use fresh herbs and freshly ground spices, but the dried and ready-ground varieties have their merits. Dried herbs and spices keep well and are cheaper – keep them in a cool, dark place, not exposed to sunlight. Using herbs when cooking at home should reduce the temptation to buy ready-made sauces. Often these types of sauces contain large amounts of sugar and additives. Some key dried herbs and spices to purchase are: bay leaves, thyme, oregano, parsley, mixed herbs, spices, ground cinnamon, cumin, ground coriander, crushed chillies, ground ginger, mixed spice, curry powder and turmeric.

Pasta Whether fresh (it can also be frozen) or dried, pasta is a versatile ingredient with which to provide the body with slow-release energy. It comes in many different sizes and shapes; from the tiny tubettini (which can be added to soups to create a more substantial dish), to penne, fusilli, rigatoni and conchiglie, up to the larger cannelloni and lasagne sheets and, of course, spaghetti. (***See also page 45.***)

Noodles Also very useful and can accompany any Far Eastern dish. They are low fat and also available in the wholemeal variety. Rice noodles are available for those who have gluten-free diets; like pasta noodles, they provide slow-release energy to the body.

Rice When cooked, rice swells to create a substantial low-fat dish. Basmati and Thai fragrant rice are well suited to Indian and Thai curries, as the fine grains absorb the sauce and their delicate creaminess balances the pungency of the spices. Arborio is only one type of risotto rice – many are available, depending on whether the risotto is meant to accompany meat, fish or vegetables. Long-grain is perhaps the most popular and versatile of rice and is perfect for both rich and simple dishes. Having a subtle flavour, it is milled to remove the husk and bran layer. On cooking, the grains separate to give a fluffy texture. Also available as brown long-grain. Easy-cook long-grain rice, both white and brown, is great for casseroles and for stuffing meat, fish and vegetables, as it holds its shape and firmness.

Pudding rice can be used in a variety of ways to create an irresistible dessert. Rice will keep for several years if kept in sealed packets.

However, it is at its best when fresh. To ensure freshness, always buy rice from reputable shops with a good turnover and buy in small quantities. Once opened, store the rice in an airtight container in a cool, dry place to keep out moisture.

Although there are quite a few varieties of rice readily available, it is not necessary to have them all. To begin with why not buy either white or brown basmati rice, Thai fragrant rice if you intend to cook a lot of stir-fries and long-grain rice, which is a versatile rice and can be used for most dishes.

Couscous Not essential, but you may like to use this occasionally. Now available in instant form, couscous just needs to be covered with boiling water, then forked. Couscous is a precooked wheat semolina. Traditional couscous needs to be steamed and is available from health food stores and supermarkets. This type of couscous contains more nutrients than the instant variety.

Bulgur wheat Also not essential. A cracked wheat that is often used in tabbouleh. Bulgur wheat is a good source of complex carbohydrate.

Pulses/beans A vital ingredient for the store cupboard, pulses – which include beans such as kidney, borlotti, cannellini, butter and flageolet, as well as split peas and lentils – are easy to store, have a very high nutritional value and are great when added to soups, casseroles, curries and hotpots. Pulses also act as a thickener, whether flavoured or on their own.

Beans come in two forms: either dried (in which case they need to be soaked overnight and then some must be boiled for 10 minutes before use – it is important to follow the instructions on the back of the packet), or canned, which although more expensive is a convenient time-saver because the preparation of dried pulses can take a while. When boiling previously dried pulses, remember that salt should not be added as this will make the skins tough and inedible. If buying canned pulses, try to buy the variety in water with no added salt or sugar. These simply need to be drained and rinsed before being added to a dish.

Dried fruit The ready-to-eat variety are particularly good as they are plump, juicy and do not need to be soaked. They are fantastic when puréed into a compote, added to water and heated to make a pie filling and when added to stuffing mixtures. They are also good cooked with meats, rice or couscous.

Flours Apart from cornflour and perhaps a little plain flour, since both are used for thickening sauces, you may not need to stock flour unless you intend to bake. It is worth mentioning that wholemeal flour should not be stored for too long at room temperature as the fats may turn rancid.

Cooking oil It is recognised that olive oil is the best oil to use both for health properties and taste. If intending only to cook with olive oil, then buy 'mild', 'medium' or 'blended for cooking' olive oil; if using it for salad dressing or to drizzle, then invest in a bottle of extra virgin olive oil too (do not cook with it).

However, there other oils which are still healthy to use and are cheaper. Try vegetable oil, which can be used for all methods of cooking, has a distinct flavour and is reasonably priced, as is sunflower oil, which is more delicate and a lighter oil. Or try rapeseed oil, corn oil or groundnut oil, which is usually used in Eastern cooking. Speciality oils, such as sesame, walnut, herb and spiced flavoured oils are expensive and are reserved mainly to add extra flavour at the end of cooking or for salad or vegetable dressings.

Stock Good-quality stock is a must in low-fat cooking, as it provides a good flavour base for many dishes. Many supermarkets now carry a variety of fresh and organic stocks, which, although they need refrigeration, are probably one of the most time- and effort-saving ingredients available. There is also a fairly large range of dried stock, perhaps the best being bouillon, a high-quality form of stock (available in powder or liquid form) which can be added to any dish, whether it be a sauce, casserole, pie or soup.

Sauce ingredients Many people favour meals that can be prepared and cooked in 30–45 minutes, so helpful ingredients that kick-start a sauce are great. A good-quality passata sauce or canned tomatoes, which are almost as good as passata but cheaper, can act as the foundation for any sauce, as can a good-quality green or red pesto (though pesto can be great to make from scratch). Other handy store cupboard additions include tapenade, mustard and anchovies. These have very distinctive tastes and are particularly flavoursome. Roasted red pepper sauce and sun-dried tomato paste, which tends to be sweeter and more intensely flavoured than regular tomato purée, are also very useful.

Vinegar This is another worthwhile store-cupboard essential and, with so many uses, it might be worth splashing out on really good-quality wine vinegar or even a balsamic vinegar.

Sauces and flavours Eastern flavourings such as fish sauce, soy sauce, red and green curry paste, chilli sauce and Chinese rice wine all offer

mouthwatering flavours to any dish. For those who are incredibly short on time, or who rarely shop, it is now possible to purchase a selection of ready-prepared freshly minced garlic, ginger and chilli (available in jars which can be kept in the refrigerator). Mustard and ketchup, which you may use in your sarnies, can also be handy in cooking.

Alcohol You are not going to be flambéing or cooking with expensive brandy, but since you may be partial to the odd glass of wine or pint of beer, then why not use any leftovers in risottos and stews?

Canned foods Canned ingredients can be just as good quality as fresh, at half the price and with a long shelf life – some are more reliable than others however. Top of the list are canned tomatoes, swiftly followed by tuna, sardines, anchovies, olives, sweetcorn, beans, baked beans and perhaps corned beef.

Cooking Eggs

No other food is as versatile in cooking as the egg – it is used in many diverse ways and is an essential ingredient for all good cooks. But first things first: here are some of the basic and essential ways to cook eggs.

Boiled Eggs

Eggs should be boiled in gently simmering water. Remove the egg from the refrigerator at least 30 minutes before cooking.

1. Bring a pan of water to the boil, then, once boiling, lower the heat to a simmer.

2. Gently lower the egg into the water and cook for 3 minutes for lightly set, or 4 minutes for a slightly firmer set.

3. Remove and lightly tap to stop the egg continuing to cook.

4. Serve lightly boiled eggs with toast or buttered bread cut into fingers to use as dippers.

Hard-boiled eggs should be cooked for 10 minutes, then plunged into cold water and left until cold before shelling.

Fried Eggs

1. Put a little sunflower oil or butter in a frying pan and heat.

2. Break an egg into a cup or small jug. Carefully slip into the pan.

3. Cook, spooning the hot oil or fat over the egg,

for 3–4 minutes until set to personal preference.

4. Remove with a palette knife or fish slice.

5. Serve with freshly grilled bacon or sausages, or on toast with baked beans and tomatoes.

Poached Eggs

1. Half-fill a frying pan with water. Bring to a gentle boil, then reduce the heat to a simmer.

2. Add either a little salt or a few drops of vinegar or lemon juice – this will help the egg to retain its shape.

3. Break the egg into a cup or small jug and carefully slip into the simmering water. Lightly oiled round, plain pastry cutters can be used to contain the eggs, if preferred.

4. Cover the pan with a lid and cook for 3–4 minutes until set to personal preference.

5. Once cooked, remove by draining with a fish slice or flat spatula.

6. Serve either on hot buttered toast or on top of sliced ham or freshly cooked spinach.

Scrambled Eggs

For sufficient scrambled eggs, allow two eggs per person.

1. Melt 1 tablespoon butter or margarine in a small pan.

2. Break the eggs into a small bowl and add 1 tablespoon milk and seasoning to taste. Whisk with a fork until blended, then pour into the melted butter or margarine.

3. Cook over a gentle heat, stirring with a wooden spoon, until set and creamy.

4. Serve on hot buttered toast with smoked salmon, if liked, or stir in some freshly snipped chives or chopped tomatoes.

Omelettes

For a basic omelette, allow two eggs per person. Add herbs and seasoning as desired.

1. Break the eggs into a small bowl, add seasoning to taste and 1 tablespoon milk. Whisk with a fork until frothy.

2. Heat 2 teaspoons oil in a frying pan and, when hot, pour in the egg mixture.

3. Cook gently, using a wooden spoon to bring the mixture from the edges of the pan to the centre and let the uncooked egg mixture flow to the edges.

4. When the egg has set, cook without moving it for an extra minute before folding the omelette into three and gently turning out onto a warmed serving plate. Take care not to overcook.

Cheese Omelette

Proceed as before, then sprinkle 25–40 g/1–1½ oz grated mature Cheddar cheese on top of the lightly set omelette. Cook for a further 2 minutes, or until the cheese starts to melt. If liked, place under a preheated grill for 2–3 minutes until golden. Fold and serve.

Tomato Omelette

Proceed as for a plain omelette. After 2 minutes of cooking time, add 1 chopped tomato on top of the omelette. Cook as above until set.

Mushroom Omelette

Wipe and slice 50 g/2 oz button mushrooms. Heat 1 tablespoon butter or margarine in a small pan and cook the mushrooms for 2–3 minutes. Drain and reserve. Cook the omelette as above, adding the mushrooms once set.

Separating Eggs

Occasionally a recipe may call for egg yolks or whites – to obtain these you need to literally separate the white from the yolk. Separate eggs as follows:

1. Crack an egg in half lightly and cleanly over a bowl, being careful not to break the yolk and keeping the yolk in the shell.

2. Tip the yolk backwards and forwards between the two shell halves, allowing as much of the white as possible to spill out into the bowl.

Keep or discard the yolk and/or the white as needed. Make sure that you do not get any yolk in your whites, as this will prevent successful whisking of the whites. It takes practice!

Cooking Rice

There are countless ways to cook rice, but much depends on the variety of rice being used, the dish being prepared and the desired results. Each variety of rice has its own characteristics. Some types of rice cook to light, separate grains, some to a rich, creamy consistency and some to a consistency where the grains stick together. Different types of rice have different powers of absorption.

Most rice (but not risotto) benefits from washing before cooking – tip into a sieve and rinse under cold running water until the water runs clear. This removes any starch still clinging to the grains.

Long-grain Rice on the Hob

The simplest method of cooking long-grain rice is to add it to plenty of boiling, salted water in a large saucepan. Allow 50 g/2 oz rice per person when cooking as an accompaniment.

1. Rinse under cold running water until clear, then tip into rapidly boiling water.

2. Stir once, then, when the water returns to the boil, reduce the heat and simmer uncovered.

3. Allow 10–12 minutes for white rice and 30–40 minutes for brown – check the packet for specific timings.

4. The easiest way to test if rice is cooked is to bite a couple of grains – they should be tender but still firm.

5. Drain immediately, then return to the pan with a little butter and herbs, if liked. Fluff up with a fork and serve.

To keep the rice warm, put it in a bowl and place over a pan of barely simmering water. Cover the top of the bowl with a dishtowel until ready to serve.

Absorption Method

Cooking rice using the absorption method is also simple. Weigh out the quantity, then measure it by volume in a measuring jug – you will need 150 ml/¼ pint for two people.

1. Rinse the rice, then tip into a large saucepan. If liked, cook the rice in a little butter or oil for 1 minute.

2. Pour in 2 parts water or stock to 1 part rice, season with salt and bring to the boil.

3. Cover, then simmer gently until the liquid is absorbed and the rice is tender. White rice will take 15 minutes to cook, whereas brown rice will take 35 minutes. If there is still a little liquid left when the rice is tender, uncover and cook for 1 minute until evaporated.

4. Remove from the heat and leave covered for 4–5 minutes, then fluff up before serving.

Oven-baked Method

The oven-baked method works by absorption too, but takes longer than cooking on the hob. For oven-baked rice for two:

1. Fry a chopped onion in 1 tablespoon olive oil in a 1.1 litre/2 pint flameproof casserole dish until soft and golden.

2. Add 75 g/3 oz long-grain rice and cook for 1 minute.

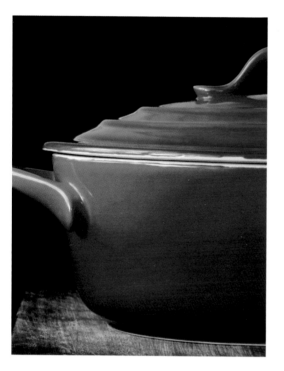

Cooking in the Microwave

1. Place the rinsed long-grain rice in a large microwaveable bowl.

2. Add boiling water or stock, allowing 300 ml/½ pint for 125 g/4 oz rice and 500 ml/18 fl oz for 225 g/8 oz rice. Add a pinch of salt and a knob of butter, if desired.

3. Cover with pierced plastic wrap and cook on high for 3 minutes.

4. Stir, re-cover and cook on medium for 12 minutes for white rice and 25 minutes for brown.

5. Leave covered for 5 minutes before fluffing up and serving.

3. Stir in 300 ml/½ pint stock – add a finely pared strip of lemon zest or a bay leaf, if liked.

4. Cover and bake in a preheated oven at 180°C/ 350°F/Gas Mark 4 for 40 minutes, or until the rice is tender and all the stock has been absorbed. Fluff up before serving.

Cooking Pasta

Though it is possible to make your own fresh pasta at home, few of us have the time or energy to do this, especially when fresh and dried pasta is so readily available to buy. In fact, although you may occasionally like to buy ready-made stuffed fresh pasta such as tortellini, there is no need to buy fresh pasta noodles or shapes – dried pasta is just as good, if not better, not to mention cheaper and long-lasting.

How to Cook Perfect Pasta

As an approximate guide, allow 75–125 g/3–4 oz uncooked pasta per person. The amount will depend on whether the pasta is being served for a light or main meal and the type of sauce that it is being served with. Follow a few simple rules to ensure that your pasta is cooked to perfection every time:

1. Choose a large saucepan – there needs to be plenty of room for the pasta to move around so it does not stick together.

2. Cook the pasta in a large quantity of fast-boiling, well-salted water, ideally 4 litres/7 pints water and 1½–2 tablespoons salt for every 350–450 g/12 oz–1 lb pasta.

3. Tip in the pasta all at once, stir and cover. Return to a rolling boil, then remove the lid. Once it is boiling, lower the heat to medium-high and cook the pasta for the required time. It should be al dente – in other words, tender but still firm to the bite.

4. Drain, reserving a little of the cooking water to stir into the drained pasta. This helps to thin the sauce, if necessary, and helps prevent the pasta sticking together as it cools.

45

Potatoes

Potatoes are invaluable; they can be boiled, baked, mashed, roasted, chipped – what would we do without them? You may just buy the first or biggest ones you come across, but it may help you to know that potatoes are classified according to how early in the season they are ready for harvesting and are named as follows: first early, second early and maincrop.

The first earlies (such as the Maris Bard variety) are the first new potatoes on the market; they are very fresh and young and the skins can simply be rubbed off. The second earlies (such as Anya) are still new potatoes, but their skins will have begun to set. These potatoes will be difficult to scrape and are better cooked in their skins. Main crop potatoes (such as Maris Piper, King Edward, Charlotte, Désirée) are available all year round and may have been stored for several months.

Choosing

When buying potatoes, always choose ones with smooth, firm skins. When purchasing new potatoes, check that they are really young and fresh by scraping the skin – it should peel away very easily. Only buy the quantity you need and use within a couple of days.

Check maincrop potatoes to make sure that they are firm and not sprouting or showing any signs of mould. Avoid buying and discard any potatoes with greenish patches or carefully cut them out. These parts of the potato are toxic and a sign that they have been stored in light.

Storing

Potatoes should be stored in a cool, dark place but not in the refrigerator as the dampness will make them sweat, causing mould to grow. If the potatoes come in plastic bags, take them out and store in a paper bag or on a vegetable rack. If you prefer to buy in bulk, keep the potatoes in a cold, dark, dry place such as a larder or garage, making sure that they do not freeze in cold weather.

Sweet potatoes should be stored in a cool, dry place but, unlike ordinary potatoes, do not need to be kept in the dark.

Which Potato for Which Method?

Generally, new potato varieties have a firm and waxy texture that does not break up during cooking, so they are ideal for boiling, steaming and salads. Maincrop potatoes, on the other hand, have a more floury texture and lend themselves to mashing and roasting. Both types are suitable for chips. Individual potato varieties have their own characteristics. Some maincrop varieties are better for boiling than baking and vice versa, so choose the most appropriate type of potato for the dish being prepared (check the label or ask your retailer).

Whichever way you choose to serve potatoes, allow 125–175 g/4–6 oz per person (about 4–6 new potatoes or 1–2 medium potatoes).

Boiled Potatoes

New Potatoes
Most of the new potatoes available nowadays are fairly clean – especially those sold in supermarkets – and simply need a light scrub before cooking in their skins.

1. If the potatoes are very dirty, use a small scrubbing brush or scourer to remove both the skins and dirt (or leave the skins on if they are second earlies, and peel when cooked, if liked).

2. Add them to a pan of cold, salted water and bring to the boil. Cover the pan with a lid and

simmer for 12–15 minutes until tender. Very firm new potatoes can be simmered for 8 minutes, then left to stand in the hot water for a further 10 minutes until cooked through.

3. Add a couple of sprigs of fresh herbs to the pan if you like – fresh mint is traditionally used to flavour potatoes.

4. Drain the potatoes thoroughly and, if you want to peel them now, hold the hot potatoes with a fork to make this easier. Serve hot, tossed in a little melted butter or, for a change, a tablespoon of pesto.

'Old' (Maincrop) Potatoes

1. Choose a maincrop potato suitable for boiling, then peel thinly and cut into even-sized pieces. Alternatively, you can cook the potatoes in their skins and peel them after cooking.

2. Add to a saucepan of cold, salted water and bring to the boil. Cover the pan with a lid and simmer for 20 minutes, or until tender. Drain. (It is particularly important to cook floury potatoes gently or the outsides may start to fall apart before they are tender in the centre. Drain the potatoes in a colander, then return them to the pan to dry out over a very low heat for 1–2 minutes.)

Mashed Potatoes

1. Boil your maincrop potatoes as described and, once cooked, roughly mash and add a knob of butter or margarine and 2 tablespoons of milk per person. Mash until smooth, with a hand masher, grater or a potato ricer.

2. Season to taste with salt, freshly ground black pepper and a little freshly grated nutmeg, if liked, then beat for a few seconds with a wooden spoon until fluffy.

As an alternative to butter or margarine, use a good-quality olive oil or crème fraîche. Finely chopped red and green chillies, crispy-cooked crumbled bacon, fresh herbs or grated Parmesan cheese can also be stirred in for additional flavour.

Steamed Potatoes

All potatoes are suitable for steaming. Floury potatoes, however, are ideal for this method of cooking, as they fall apart easily when boiled.

1. New and small potatoes can be steamed whole, but larger ones should be cut into even-sized pieces.

2. Place the potatoes in a steamer, colander or sieve over boiling water and cover. Steam for 10 minutes if the potatoes are very small or, if they are cut into large chunks, cook for 20–25 minutes.

Chips

You are unlikely to deep-fry your own chips – ideally you'd need a deep-fat fryer; and lots of hot oil can be dangerous to use and onerous to replace. Of course you can buy frozen oven chips, but how about baking your own? It's lower fat than frying and less hassle.

1. Preheat the oven to 200°C/400°F/Gas Mark 6 and place a nonstick baking tray in the oven to heat up.

2. Cut the potatoes into 1.5 cm/$^5/_8$ inch slices, then cut the slices into long strips about 1.5 cm/$^5/_8$ inch wide to create classic chips, or cut your potatoes into chunky wedges, if preferred. Put the chips or wedges in a pan of cold water and quickly bring to the boil.

3. Simmer for 2 minutes, then drain in a colander. Leave for a few minutes to dry.

4. Drizzle over 1$^1/_2$–2 tablespoons of olive or sunflower oil and toss to coat.

5. Tip onto the heated baking tray and cook in the preheated oven for 20–25 minutes, turning occasionally, until golden brown and crisp.

Sautéed Potatoes

1. Cut peeled potatoes into rounds about 0.5 cm/ ¹/₄ inch thick and pat dry.

2. Heat 25 g/1 oz/2 tbsp unsalted butter or margarine and 2 tablespoons oil in a large heavy-based frying pan until hot.

3. Add the potatoes in a single layer and cook for 4–5 minutes until the undersides are golden.

4. Turn with a large fish slice/spatula and gently cook the other side for 12–15 minutes until golden and tender.

5. Drain on paper towels and sprinkle with a little salt before serving.

Baked Potatoes

Allow a large (300–375 g/11–13 oz) potato per person and, if you can, choose a variety such as Maris Piper, Cara, King Edward, Russet Burbank or Russet Arcadia.

1. Wash and dry the potatoes, prick the skins lightly, then rub each one with a little oil and sprinkle with salt.

2. Bake at 200°C/400°F/Gas Mark 6 for 1–1¹/₂ hours until the skins are crisp and the centres are very soft. To speed up the cooking time, thread onto metal skewers, as this conducts heat to the middle of the potatoes.

Roast Potatoes

For crisp and brown outsides and fluffy centres, choose potatoes suitable for baking.

1. Thinly peel the potatoes and cut into even-sized pieces.

2. Drop into a pan of boiling, salted water and simmer for 5 minutes.

3. Turn off the heat and leave for a further 3–4 minutes.

4. Drain well and return the potatoes to the pan over a low heat for a minute to dry them and to roughen the edges.

5. Carefully transfer them to a roasting tin containing hot oil. Baste well, then bake at 220°C/425°F/Gas Mark 7 for 20 minutes.

6. Turn them and cook for a further 20–30 minutes, turning and basting at least one more time. Serve as soon as the potatoes are ready.

Microwaving Potatoes

The microwave can be used to boil new potatoes or peeled chunks of potato as follows:

1. To cook new potatoes in the microwave, prick the skins with a skewer to prevent them from bursting.

2. Place in a microwaveable bowl with 3 tablespoons boiling water.

3. Cover with clingfilm which has been pierced 2–3 times and cook on High for 12–15 minutes until tender.

You can also 'bake' potatoes in the microwave, providing you do not want the skins to be crispy:

1. Place each potato on a circle of paper towels. Make several cuts in each to ensure that the skins do not burst.

2. Transfer to the microwave plate and cook on High for 4–6 minutes per potato, allowing an extra 3–4 minutes for every additional potato. Turn the potatoes at least once during cooking.

3. Leave to stand for 5 minutes before serving.

Alternatively, get the best of both worlds by starting them off in the microwave for 4 minutes and then finishing them to a nice baked finish in the oven for 10–12 minutes. It may take rather longer if they are very big.

Meat, Poultry & Fish

Red Meat

Meat can be expensive, and, although it offers an excellent source of protein, B vitamins and iron, it also contains saturated fatty acids which are linked to raised blood cholesterol levels and increased risk of coronary heart disease. For this reason, it is now recommended that red meat is only eaten 2–3 times per week. Nonetheless, as a student you do not have to forego meat by any means.

Cost

Home-grown meat is normally more expensive than imported meat. Meat also varies in price, depending on the cut: the more expensive and tender meats are usually those cuts that exercised less. They need a minimal amount of cooking and are suitable for roasting, grilling, griddling, frying and stir-frying. The cheaper cuts, which are the belly, shoulder, neck, stewing meat (chuck or skirt, which is often sold as mince) and breast, such as lamb's, need longer, slower cooking and are used in casseroles and stews and for slow roasting. If you compare the price of mince made from skirt to the price of mince made from steak, such as rump, there is a big difference, but the cheaper skirt mince contains a lot of fat which needs cooking out.

Choosing

Look for meat that is lean without an excess of fat, is a good colour and has no unpleasant odour. If in doubt about the suitability of a cut, ask the butcher, who should be happy to advise.

Frozen Meat

If buying frozen meat, allow to thaw before using. This is especially important for both pork and poultry

Beef

When choosing beef, look for meat that is a good vibrant, uniform colour, with creamy yellow fat. There should be small flecks of fat (marbling) throughout, as this helps the meat to be tender. Avoid meat with excess gristle. Bright red beef means that the animal has been butchered recently, whereas meat that has been hung in a traditional manner should be a deep, dark ruby red, almost purple. The darker the colour, especially with roasting joints, the more tender and succulent the beef will be.

Lamb

Lamb is probably at its best in the spring, when the youngest lamb is available. It is tender to eat, with a delicate flavour, and its flesh is a paler pink than the older lamb, where the flesh is more red. The colour of the fat is also a good indication of age: young lamb fat is a very light, creamy colour. As the lamb matures, the fat becomes whiter and firmer. Imported lamb also has firmer, whiter fat. Lamb is naturally a fattier meat than beef, so take care when choosing. It used

(covered later). It is better to thaw meat slowly, lightly covered on the bottom shelf of the refrigerator. Use within 2–3 days of thawing, providing it has been kept in the refrigerator. If buying meat to freeze, do not freeze large joints in a home freezer, as it will not be frozen quickly enough.

Storing

Store thawed or fresh meat out of the supermarket wrappings, on a plate, lightly covered with greaseproof or baking paper and then wrap with clingfilm, if liked. Do not secure the paper tightly round the meat, as it needs to breathe. Ensure that the raw meat juices do not drip onto cooked foods. The refrigerator needs to be at a temperature of 5°C/40°F. Fresh meat such as joints, chops and steaks can be stored for up to 3 days. Minced meats, sausages and offal should be stored for only 1 day.

to be possible to buy mutton (lamb that is at least one year old), but this now tends to be available only in specialist outlets. It has a far stronger, almost gamey flavour and the joints tend to be larger.

Pork

Pork should be pale pink in colour and slightly marbled with small flecks of fat. There should be a layer of firm white fat with a thin elastic skin (rind), which can be scored before roasting to provide crackling. All cuts of pork are tender, as the pigs are slaughtered at an early age and are reared to be lean rather than fatty. Pork used to be well cooked, if not overcooked, due to the danger of the parasite trichina. This no longer applies, however, and it is now recommended that the meat is cooked less to keep it moist and tender.

Bacon, Gammon and Ham

Bacon and gammon are cured pork produced by injections of brine as well as immersion in brine or salt. The meat becomes a much paler pink with creamy white fat and rind. For smoked bacon, the meat is smoked after it is cured, which produces the darker brown rind and meat. Another name for unsmoked bacon is 'green' bacon, although this term is not used as much these days. Before cooking, it is often soaked in cold water in order to remove some of the salt. Cuts of bacon vary according to regions and in some areas, bacon is called ham.

Poultry

'Poultry' relates to turkey, chicken, poussin, duck and goose. It is low in saturated fat and is a good source of protein. Remove the skin before eating to keep it low-fat. Most is sold plucked, drawn and trussed.

Welfare

Due to intensive farming used since the Second World War, chicken in particular offers a good source of cheap meat. However, there is a growing movement to return to the more traditional methods of farming, for better quality and better animal welfare. Free-range and organically grown chickens offer a far more succulent bird with excellent flavour, although they tend to be more expensive.

Cooking

Ensure that poultry is thoroughly cooked and the juices run clear. Rest for 10 minutes before carving. Use within 2 days of cooking.

Fish and Seafood

Requiring only minimal cooking, all fish is an excellent choice for speedy and nutritious meals. There are two categories of fish: white and oily. The remaining types of seafood can be divided into three categories: shellfish, crustaceans and molluscs.

Buying

Both home-grown and imported poultry, fresh and frozen are available. When buying fresh poultry, look for plump birds with a flexible breast bone, and no unpleasant odour or green tinge. Frozen poultry should be rock hard with no ice crystals, as this could mean that the bird has thawed and been re-frozen. Avoid any produce where the packaging is damaged.

Thawing and Storing

When thawing, place in the refrigerator on a large plate and ensure that none of the juices drip onto other foods. Once thawed, remove all packaging, remove the giblets, if any, and reserve separately. Place on a plate and cover lightly. Use within 2 days. Treat fresh poultry the same way.

Buying and Storing Seafood

Both types of fish are sold fresh or frozen as small whole fish, fillets or cutlets. Store as soon as possible in the refrigerator. Remove from the wrappings, place on a plate, cover lightly and store towards the top. Use within one day of purchase. If using frozen, thaw slowly in the refrigerator and use within one day of thawing.

Seafood should be eaten as fresh as possible. Live seafood gives the best flavour, as long as it is consumed on the day of purchase (and cleaned thoroughly). If live is not available, buy from a reputable source and eat on the day of purchase, refrigerating until required.

White Fish

White fish such as cod, haddock, plaice or coley are an excellent source of protein and have a low fat content. They also contain vitamin B12 and niacin, plus important minerals such as phosphorous, iodine, selenium and potassium.

Oily Fish

Oily fish such as sardines, mackerel, salmon and herring have a higher fat content than white fish, but are an excellent source of Omega-3 polyunsaturated fatty acids, important in fighting heart disease, cancers and arthritis. Oily fish also contain niacin, B6, B12 and D vitamins, and the minerals selenium, iodine, potassium and phosphorous. The taste is stronger and more robust, enabling stronger flavours such as chilli and garlic to be used. It is recommended that at least two portions of oily fish should be eaten each week.

Other Kinds of Seafood

Shellfish include crustaceans, such as lobsters, which have hard shells that they shed and replace during their lifetime, and molluscs, which are animals that have hinged shells, such as scallops, or single shells, such as whelks. Other seafood includes cephalopods, such as squid, cuttlefish and octopus.

Vegetables & Salads

Vegetables add colour, texture, flavour and valuable nutrients to a meal. They play an important role in the diet, providing necessary vitamins, minerals and fibre. Vegetables are versatile: they can be served as an accompaniment to other dishes – they go well with meat, poultry and fish – or they can be used as the basis for the whole meal.

Buying

When buying fresh vegetables, always look for ones that are bright and feel firm to the touch, and avoid any that are damaged or bruised. Choose onions and garlic that are hard and not sprouting; avoid ones that are soft, as they may be damaged. Salad leaves and other leaf vegetables should be fresh, bright and crisp – do not buy any that are wilted, look limp or have yellow leaves.

Storing

Many vegetables can be kept in a cool, dry, dark place, but some should be refrigerated.

Root vegetables, tubers and winter squashes These should be kept in a cool, dry, dark place that is free of frost, such as a larder or garage. Winter squashes can be kept for several months if stored correctly.

Green vegetables, fruit vegetables and salad leaves These should be kept in the salad drawer of the refrigerator.

Vegetables such as peas and beans These do not keep for very long, so try to eat them as soon as possible after buying or picking.

Preparing

Always clean vegetables thoroughly before using. Brush or scrape off any dirt and wash well in cold water. Prepare the vegetables just before cooking, as once peeled, they lose nutrients. Do not leave them in water, as valuable water-soluble vitamins will be lost.

Lettuce and other salad Wash leaves gently under cold running water and pull off and discard any tough stalks or outer leaves. Tear rather than cut the leaves. Dry thoroughly in a salad spinner or on paper towels before use, otherwise the leaves tend to wilt.

Spinach This should be washed thoroughly to remove all traces of dirt. Cut off and discard any tough stalks and damaged leaves.

Leeks These need to be thoroughly cleaned before use to remove any grit and dirt. After trimming the root and tough ends, make one cut lengthways (but not all the way along if you are intending to cook whole), and rinse under running water, getting right between the leaves.

Mushrooms Since mushrooms have a high water content, it is generally advised not to wash them, in order to avoid them absorbing even more water. Therefore, most mushrooms can just be wiped with paper towels or a damp cloth.

Cooking Techniques

Vegetables can be cooked in a variety of different ways, such as baking, barbecuing, blanching, boiling, braising, deep-frying, grilling, roasting, sautéing, steaming and stir-frying.

Boiling
Always cook vegetables in a minimum amount of water and do not overcook, or valuable nutrients will be lost. It is best to cut vegetables into even-sized pieces and cook them briefly.

Blanching and Parboiling
These mean lightly cooking raw vegetables for a brief period of time, whether parboiling potatoes before roasting (see pages 50–51), cooking cabbage before braising or cooking leaf vegetables such as spinach. Spinach should be cooked in only the water clinging to its leaves for 2–3 minutes until

wilted. Blanching is also used to remove skins easily from tomatoes. Cut a small cross in the top of the tomato and place in a heatproof bowl. Cover with boiling water and leave for a few seconds, then drain and peel off the skin.

Braising

This method is a slow way of cooking certain vegetables, notably red or white cabbage. The vegetable is simmered for a long period of time in a small amount of stock or water.

Steaming

This is a great way to cook vegetables such as broccoli, cauliflower, beans, carrots, parsnips and peas.

1. Cut the vegetables into even-sized pieces. Fill a large saucepan with about 5 cm/2 inches water, bring to the boil, then reduce to a simmer.

2. Place the vegetables in a metal steamer basket or colander and lower into the saucepan, then cover and steam until tender. Alternatively, use a plate standing on a trivet in the pan. Asparagus is traditionally cooked in an asparagus steamer. Do not let the water boil – it should just simmer.

3. Once tender, serve – there is no need to drain!

Microwaving

Vegetables can be cooked very successfully in the microwave and they retain all their flavour and nutrients as well as their colour.

1. Prepare the vegetables, cutting into even-sized pieces. Place in a microwaveable bowl or arrange in a shallow dish.

2. For firm vegetables such as root vegetables, add 1–3 tablespoons water and cover with clingfilm. Pierce in a couple of places. Cook on high for 2–4 minutes, depending on how many vegetables and which variety are being cooked. The more delicate vegetables will require less cooking time and less water. Refer to manufacturer's guidelines to be sure of times.

3. Remove from the oven and leave to stand for 1–2 minutes before serving. Do not season until after cooking, especially with salt, as this will toughen the vegetables.

Grilling

To grill peppers, cut in half or quarters and discard the seeds. Place, skin side uppermost on a foil-lined rack. Brush lightly with a little oil, then cook under the preheated grill for 5 minutes. Turn over, brush again and continue to grill for a further 3 minutes or until tender. Serve.

To grill aubergines, trim and wash, then either cut into slices or lengths. Brush lightly with a little oil and place on a foil-lined grill rack. Cook under the preheated grill for 3–5 minutes or until the aubergine has softened. Turn over, brush again and continue grilling for a further 3 minutes or until tender.

To grill tomatoes, rinse and cut in half. Place on a foil-lined grill rack and, if liked, season to taste. Cook under a preheated grill and cook for 3–5 minutes until cooked to personal preference.

Grilling to Remove Skin

To remove the skins from peppers:

1. Cut in half lengthways and deseed. Place skin-side up on the grill rack under a preheated hot grill and cook until the skins are blackened.

2. Remove with tongs and place in a polythene bag. Seal and leave for 8–10 minutes, until the peppers are cool enough to handle.

3. Once cool, remove from the bag and carefully peel away the blackened skin.

Stir-frying

Stir-frying is an excellent way of serving all manner of vegetables. This way, all the nutrients are retained due to the short cooking time. Vegetables suitable for stir-frying are: peppers, courgettes, sugar snap peas, beans, baby corn, carrots, pak choi, spinach, tiny broccoli florets, spring onions and mushrooms, as well as sprouting seeds and shoots. To stir-fry:

1. Prepare all the vegetables before starting to cook. Peel, trim then cut any large pieces of vegetables into thin strips.

2. Heat a wok or frying pan for 1 minute or until very hot, then add 1–2 tablespoons oil and carefully swirl the pan with the hot oil.

3. Add spices and flavours such as grated root ginger, chopped chilli and lemon grass and cook for 1 minute, then add the prepared vegetables, starting with the firmest, such as carrot.

4. Using a large spatula or spoon, stir-fry over a high heat, adding soy or other sauce as required.

Cook for about 3–4 minutes, ensuring that the vegetables are still crisp.

Sweating

This method cooks vegetables such as onions in their own juices with or without a little oil. The vegetables should not be browned by this method and will retain masses of flavour and nutrients.

1. Prepare and clean the vegetables and cut into even-sized pieces.

2. Place in a frying pan or large saucepan over a low heat, with a little oil, if liked.

3. Cover with a lid and cook very gently in the steam that is generated. Stir occasionally. Use either in a casserole or as the basis for a soup or sauce.

Frying

This method relates to cooking vegetables in oil. It can be either shallow frying or deep frying (see also page 50 for sautéing). Shallow frying uses a minimal amount of oil whereas with deep frying the vegetables are plunged into hot oil.

To shallow fry:

1. Prepare the vegetables and cut into even-sized pieces. Heat some oil in a frying pan and add the vegetables.

2. Fry over a medium heat for 12–15 minutes until cooked and golden.

To deep fry:

1. Prepare the vegetables and cut into even sized pieces. Half fill a deep fryer, large saucepan or wok with oil such as sunflower or vegetable oil. Heat to 180°C/350°F or when a small cube of bread turns golden in 30 seconds.

2. Place the food to be fried in the frying basket or on a wide, flat slotted spoon and carefully lower into the hot oil. Take care if the food is slightly wet as it may spit.

3. Cook for 5–10 minutes until the food is golden and cooked. Drain on kitchen paper and serve.

Roasting

Suitable for vegetables such as fennel, courgettes, pumpkin, squash, peppers, garlic, aubergines, potatoes, onions and tomatoes. Cut the vegetables into even-sized chunks. Heat some oil in a roasting tin in a preheated oven at 200°C/400°F/Gas Mark 6. Put the vegetables in the hot oil, baste and roast in the oven for 30 minutes. Garlic can be split into different cloves or whole heads can be roasted. It is best not to peel them until cooked.

Soups

Pumpkin Soup

MAKES 1 PORTION

175 g/6 oz pumpkin flesh
  (after peeling and
  discarding the seeds), cut
  into 2.5 cm/1 inch cubes
1 tbsp olive or sunflower oil
1 small onion, peeled
1 small leek, trimmed

1 small carrot, peeled
1 small celery stalk
1 garlic clove, peeled
  and crushed
450 ml/¾ pint water
salt and freshly ground
  black pepper

freshly grated nutmeg,
  to taste
2 tbsp milk
cayenne pepper, to taste
  (optional)
1 tbsp single cream (optional)
warm herby bread, to serve

Heat the oil in a large saucepan and cook the pumpkin for 2–3 minutes, coating it in the oil.
Chop the onion and leek finely and cut the carrot and celery into small dice. Add the vegetables
to the saucepan with the garlic and cook, stirring, for 5 minutes or until they have begun to
soften. Cover with the water and bring to the boil. Season with plenty of salt and pepper and
the nutmeg, cover and simmer for 15–20 minutes until all of the vegetables are tender.

Remove from the heat, cool slightly then blend to a smooth purée using a handheld blender (or
a food processor or liquidizer if you have one). Pass through a sieve into a clean saucepan.
Adjust the seasoning to taste and add the milk with sufficient water to obtain the correct
consistency. Bring the soup to boiling point, add the cayenne pepper, if using, and serve
immediately swirled with the cream, if using, with warm herby bread.

Store any remaining soup, when cool, in the fridge in a bowl covered with clingfilm or pour into
a small freezer bag placed in a wide-mouth jar and freeze for 4 hours or until solid. Remove
from the jar and secure the bag, label and date. Use within 1 month. The soup is easily
thawed: simply place the bag in the saucepan you will use for reheating and leave for about 6
hours or overnight. To reheat, tip the contents of the bag into the pan and heat over a gentle
heat, stirring frequently. Add a little extra milk if too thick. Heat until piping hot.

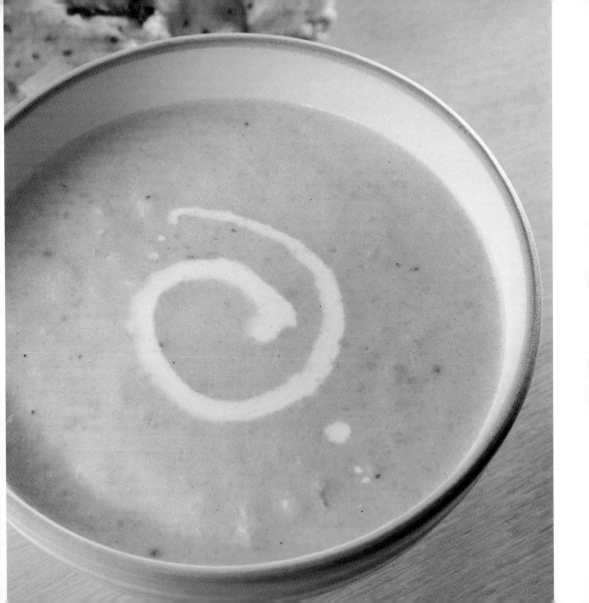

Curried Parsnip Soup

MAKES 1 PORTION

1 tsp olive or sunflower oil
1 small onion, peeled
   and chopped
1 garlic clove, peeled
   and crushed
½–1 tsp medium/hot
   curry powder

1 cinnamon stick (optional)
175 g/6 oz parsnips, peeled
   and chopped
450 ml/¾ pint
   vegetable stock
salt and freshly ground
   black pepper

1 tbsp low-fat natural
   yogurt, to serve
fresh coriander leaves,
   to garnish (optional)

Heat the oil in a saucepan. Cook the onion until softened and starting to turn golden.

Add the garlic, curry powder to taste and cinnamon stick, if using, to the pan. Continue to cook for a further 2 minutes, stirring frequently.

Add the parsnips and stir well. Pour in the stock and bring to the boil. Cover and simmer for 15 minutes or until the parsnips are cooked.

Allow the soup to cool. Once cooled, remove the cinnamon stick, if used, and discard.

Blend the soup with a handheld blender until very smooth. Reheat gently. Season to taste with salt and pepper. Garnish with fresh coriander, if using, and serve immediately with the yogurt.

Store any remaining soup, when cool, in the fridge in a bowl covered with clingfilm or pour into a small freezer bag placed in a wide-mouth jar and freeze for 4 hours or until solid. Remove from the jar and secure the bag, label and date. Use within 1 month (*see* page 64 for reheating instructions).

FOOD FACT

Parsnips vary in colour from pale yellow to a creamy white. They are at their best when they are the size of a large carrot. If larger, remove the central core, which can be woody.

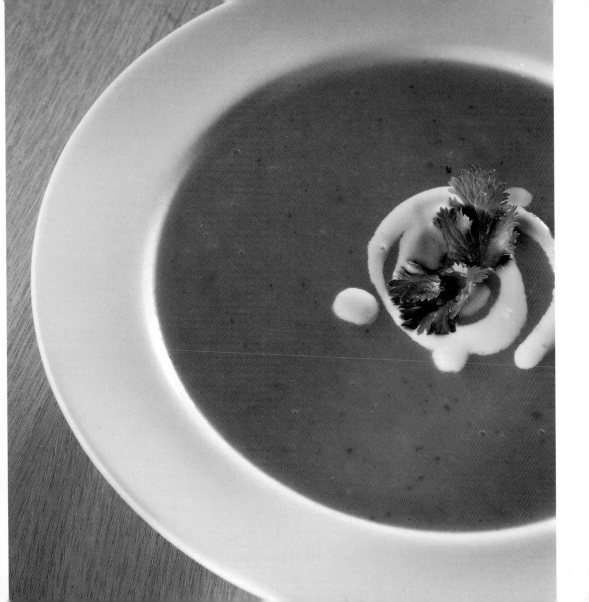

Carrot & Ginger Soup

MAKES 1 PORTION

1–2 slices of bread, crusts removed (optional)
1 tsp yeast extract (optional)
2 tsp olive oil
1 small onion, peeled and chopped
1 garlic clove, peeled and crushed
½–1 tsp ground ginger

225 g/8 oz carrots, peeled and chopped
450 ml/¾ pint vegetable stock
2.5 cm/1 inch piece of root ginger, peeled and finely grated or an extra 1 tsp ground ginger

salt and freshly ground black pepper
1 tbsp lemon juice

To garnish:
chives (optional)
lemon zest (optional)

If making the croutons, preheat the oven to 180°C/350°F/Gas Mark 4. Roughly chop the bread. Dissolve the yeast extract in 2 tablespoons of warm water and mix with the bread. Spread the bread cubes over a lightly oiled baking tray and bake for 20 minutes, turning halfway through. Remove from the oven and reserve.

Heat the oil in a large saucepan. Gently cook the onion and garlic for 3–4 minutes. Stir in the ground ginger and cook for 1 minute to release the flavour. Add the chopped carrots, then stir in the stock and the fresh ginger, if using. Simmer gently for 15 minutes.

Remove from the heat and allow to cool a little. Blend until smooth, then season to taste with salt and pepper. Stir in the lemon juice. Garnish with the croutons, chives and lemon zest, if using, and serve immediately.

If wishing to keep the soup for the next day, pour into a bowl, cover with clingfilm and store when cool in the fridge. Reheat gently stirring frequently until piping hot.

Roasted Red Pepper, Tomato & Red Onion Soup

MAKES 1 PORTION

fine spray olive or
   sunflower oil
1 small red pepper, deseeded
   and roughly chopped
1 small red onion, peeled
   and roughly chopped

125 g/4 oz tomatoes, halved
1 small crusty French loaf
1 garlic clove, peeled
300 ml/½ pint
   vegetable stock

salt and freshly ground
   black pepper
1 tsp Worcestershire sauce
   (optional)
1 tbsp half-fat fromage frais
   (optional)

Preheat the oven to 190°C/375°F/Gas Mark 5. Spray a large roasting tin with the oil and place the pepper and onion in the base. Cook in the oven for 10 minutes. Add the tomatoes and cook for a further 20 minutes or until the pepper is soft.

Cut the bread into slices. Cut the garlic clove in half and rub the cut edge of the garlic over the bread. Place all the bread slices on a large baking tray, and bake in the preheated oven for 10 minutes, turning halfway through, until golden and crisp.

Remove the vegetables from the oven and allow to cool slightly, then blend with a handheld blender until smooth. Strain the vegetable mixture through a large nylon sieve into a saucepan, to remove the seeds and skin. Add the stock, season to taste with salt and pepper and stir to mix. Heat the soup gently until piping hot.

If using the Worcestershire sauce and fromage frais place in a small bowl and beat together until smooth. Pour the soup into a warmed bowl and swirl with the fromage frais mixture. Serve immediately with the garlic toasts.

Store any remaining soup, when cool, in the fridge in a bowl covered with clingfilm or pour into a freezer bag placed in a wide-mouth jar and freeze for 4 hours or until solid. Remove from the jar, secure the bag, label and date. Use within 1 month (*see* page 64 for reheating instructions).

Tuna Chowder

MAKES 1 PORTION

2 tsp olive or sunflower oil
1 small onion, peeled and
    finely chopped
1 celery stalk, trimmed and
    finely sliced
2 tsp plain flour
300 ml/½ pint milk

100 g/3½ oz canned tuna
    in water
50 g/2 oz canned or thawed
    frozen sweetcorn, drained
1 tsp freshly chopped thyme
salt and freshly ground
    black pepper

pinch cayenne pepper
    (optional)
1 tsp freshly chopped
    parsley (optional)

TASTY TIP

To make this soup even more
colourful replace the canned
sweetcorn with a chopped
tomato. For a more filling
soup add 125 g/4 oz of
cooked chopped potatoes
for extra flavour.

TASTY TIP

Use equivalent amounts of
cooked chopped chicken
instead of the tuna. For a
creamy taste add a spoonful
of low-fat crème fraîche to the
top of the soup.

Heat the oil in a medium heavy-based saucepan. Add the onion and celery and gently cook for about 5 minutes, stirring from time to time until the onion is softened.

Stir in the flour and cook, stirring for 1 minute.

Draw the pan off the heat and gradually pour in the milk, stirring throughout.

Add the tuna and its liquid, the drained sweetcorn and the thyme.

Mix gently, then bring to the boil. Cover and simmer for 5 minutes.

Remove the pan from the heat and season to taste with salt and pepper. Sprinkle with cayenne pepper, if using, and chopped parseley, if using, and serve immediately.

Store any remaining soup, when cool, in the fridge in a bowl covered with clingfilm and use the next day. This soup will not freeze well.

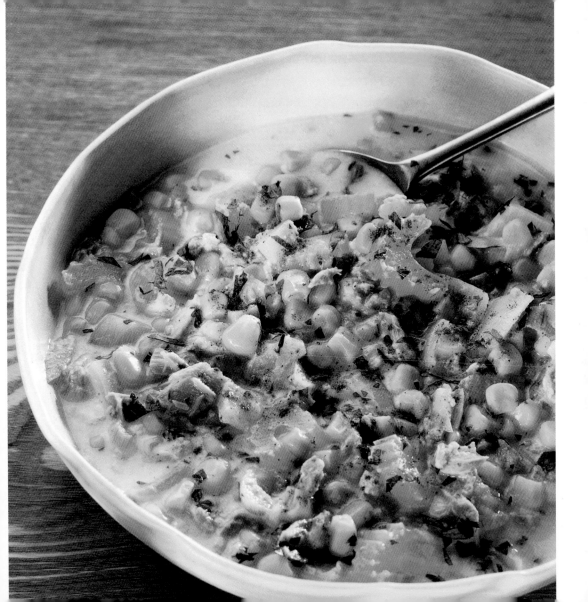

Swede, Turnip, Parsnip & Potato Soup

MAKES 1 PORTION

1 medium onion, peeled
2 tsp butter or margarine
1 small carrot, peeled and
   roughly chopped
75 g/3 oz swede, peeled and
   roughly chopped
1 small turnip, peeled and
   roughly chopped

1 small parsnip, peeled and
   roughly chopped
1 medium potato, peeled
450 ml/¾ pint
   vegetable stock
½ tsp freshly grated
   nutmeg (optional)

salt and freshly ground
   black pepper
1 tbsp vegetable oil,
   for frying
50 ml/2 fl oz milk
warm crusty bread, to serve

Finely slice the onion. Melt the butter or margarine in a medium saucepan and add half the onion with the carrot, swede, turnip, parsnip and potato. Cover and cook very gently for about 10 minutes, without colouring. Stir occasionally during this time. Add the stock and season to taste with the nutmeg, if using, and salt and pepper. Cover and bring to the boil, then reduce the heat and simmer gently for 15–20 minutes, or until the vegetables are tender. Remove from the heat and leave to cool for 30 minutes.

Heat the oil in a heavy-based frying pan. Add the remaining onion and cook over a medium heat, for about 2–3 minutes, stirring frequently, until golden brown. Remove the onion with a slotted spoon and drain well on absorbent kitchen paper. As it cools, it will turn crispy.

Pour the cooled soup into a food processor, or use a handheld blender, and process to form a smooth purée. Return to the cleaned pan, adjust the seasoning, then stir in the milk. Gently reheat and top with the crispy onions. Serve immediately with chunks of bread.

Store any remaining soup, when cool, in the fridge in a bowl covered with clingfilm or pour into a small freezer bag placed in a wide-mouth jar and freezer for 4 hours or until solid. Remove from the jar and secure the bag, label and date. Use within 1 month (*see* page 64 for reheating instructions).

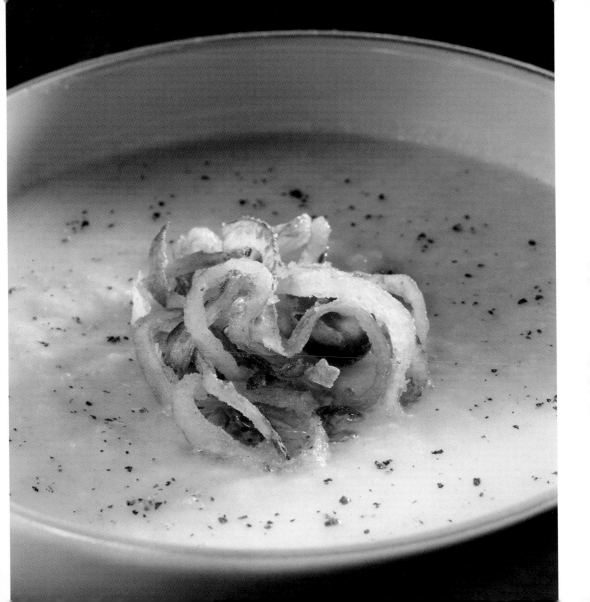

Potato, Leek & Rosemary Soup

MAKES 1 PORTION

1 tbsp butter or margarine
1 leek, trimmed and
    finely sliced
1 medium potato, peeled
    and roughly chopped

300 ml/½ vegetable stock
1 fresh rosemary sprig
150 ml/¼ pint milk
1 tsp freshly
    chopped parsley

1 tsp crème fraîche
    (optional)
salt and freshly ground
    black pepper
wholemeal rolls, to serve

Melt the butter or margarine in a medium saucepan, add the leek and cook gently for 5 minutes, stirring frequently. If liked, remove 1 tablespoon of the cooked leeks and reserve for garnishing.

Add the potato, vegetable stock, rosemary sprig and milk. Bring to the boil, then reduce the heat, cover and simmer gently for 20–25 minutes, or until the vegetables are tender.

Cool for 10 minutes. Discard the rosemary, then pour into a food processor or use a handheld blender and blend well to form a smooth-textured soup.

Return the soup to the cleaned saucepan and stir in the chopped parsley and crème fraîche, if using. Season to taste with salt and pepper. If the soup is too thick, stir in a little more milk or water. Reheat gently without boiling, then ladle into a warm soup bowl. Garnish the soup with the reserved leeks and serve immediately with wholemeal rolls.

Store any remaining soup, when cool, in the fridge in a bowl covered with clingfilm or pour into a small freezer bag placed in a wide-mouth jar and freezer for 4 hours or until solid. Remove from the jar and secure the bag, label and date. Use within 1 month (see page 64 for reheating instructions).

TASTY TIP

It is important to use fresh rosemary rather than dried for this recipe. If unavailable, use 2 bay leaves, or add a bruised fresh lemon grass stalk for a delicate flavour.

HELPFUL HINT

Make sure that the leek is thoroughly washed before using. Use as much of the darker green part of the leek as possible to give a vibrant colour.

Italian Bean Soup

MAKES 1 PORTION

2 tsp olive or sunflower oil
1 small leek, washed
    and chopped
1 garlic clove, peeled
    and crushed
1 tsp dried oregano
25 g/1 oz green beans,
    trimmed and cut into
    bite-size pieces

50 g/2 oz canned cannellini
    beans, drained and
    rinsed (or 25 g/1 oz dried
    beans if preferred –
    see Helpful Hint)
40 g/1½ oz small
    pasta shapes
450 ml/¾ pint
    vegetable stock

4 cherry tomatoes
salt and freshly ground
    black pepper
freshly shredded basil
    leaves (optional)

If using dried beans, soak them overnight in a bowl covered with water. The next day, rinse then place in a saucepan and cover with fresh water. Bring to the boil, reduce to a gentle boil and cook for 10 minutes. Drain, rinse and return to the pan. Cover with cold water, bring to the boil, reduce to a simmer and cook covered with a lid for 1–1½ hours or until tender. Drain and use as required.

Heat the oil in a medium saucepan. Add the leek, garlic and oregano and cook gently for 5 minutes, stirring occasionally. Stir in the green beans and the cannellini or cooked dried beans. Sprinkle in the pasta and pour in the stock. Bring the stock mixture to the boil, then reduce the heat to a simmer. Cook for 12–15 minutes or until the vegetables are tender and the pasta is cooked to *al dente*. Stir occasionally.

In a heavy-based frying pan, dry-fry the tomatoes over a high heat until they soften and begin to blacken. Gently crush the tomatoes in the pan with the back of a spoon and add to the soup. Season to taste with salt and pepper. Stir in the shredded basil and serve immediately.

Store any remaining soup, when cool, in the fridge in a bowl covered with clingfilm and use within 3 days. This soup will freeze, but add more basil when reheating.

HELPFUL HINT

For a change use dried beans such as haricot beans. Dried beans are cheaper than canned and are easy to use, but it takes a little foresight – you have to soak them overnight!

Rice & Tomato Soup

MAKES 1 PORTION

25 g/1 oz easy-cook
   basmati rice
2 canned tomatoes plus
   1 tbsp of juice
1 garlic clove, peeled
   and crushed
1 tsp grated lemon or
   lime zest

1 tsp olive or sunflower oil
pinch sugar
salt and freshly ground
   black pepper
300 ml/½ pint vegetable
   stock or water, boiling

For the croutons:
2 tsp ready-made pesto
   sauce
2 tsp olive or sunflower oil
2 slices ciabatta bread, cut
   into 1 cm/½ inch cubes

Preheat the oven to 220°C/425°F/Gas Mark 7. Rinse and drain the basmati rice. Chop the canned tomatoes and place with their juice in a medium heavy-based saucepan with the garlic, lime or lemon zest, oil and sugar. Season to taste with salt and pepper. Bring to the boil, then reduce the heat, cover and simmer for 10 minutes.

Add the boiling vegetable stock or water and the rice, then cook, uncovered, for a further 15–20 minutes, or until the rice is tender. If the soup is too thick, add a little more water. Reserve and keep warm, if the croutons are not ready.

Meanwhile, to make the croutons, mix the pesto and oil in a bowl. Add the bread cubes and toss until they are coated completely with the mixture. Spread on a baking sheet and bake in the preheated oven for 10–15 minutes, until golden and crisp, turning them over halfway through cooking. Serve the soup immediately sprinkled with the warm croutons.

Store any remaining soup, when cool, in the fridge in a bowl covered with clingfilm and use within 1–2 days. Do not freeze.

HELPFUL HINT

When using part of a can of food such as here with the canned tomatoes, spoon the remaining food into a small bowl or container, cover with clingfilm or lid and store in the refrigerator for up to 3 days.

Bacon & Split Pea Soup

MAKES 1 PORTION

25 g/1 oz dried split peas
1 tsp butter or margarine
1 garlic clove, peeled and
   finely chopped
1 small onion, peeled
   and thinly sliced
25 g/1 oz long-grain rice

1–2 tsp tomato purée
450 ml/¾ pint vegetable
   or chicken stock
1 small carrot, peeled and
   finely diced
2–3 rashers streaky bacon,
   finely chopped

salt and freshly ground
   black pepper
1 tsp freshly
   chopped parsley
1 tbsp single cream or milk
warm crusty garlic bread,
   to serve

Cover the dried split peas with plenty of cold water, cover loosely and leave to soak for a minimum of 12 hours, preferably overnight.

Melt the butter or margarine in a heavy-based saucepan, add the garlic and onion and cook for 2–3 minutes, without colouring. Add the rice, drained split peas and tomato purée and cook for 2–3 minutes, stirring constantly to prevent sticking. Add the stock, bring to the boil, then reduce the heat and simmer for 20–25 minutes until the rice and peas are tender. Remove from the heat and leave to cool. Blend about three-quarters of the soup in a separate bowl with a handheld blender to form a smooth purée. Pour the purée into the remaining soup in the pan. Add the carrot and cook for a further 10–12 minutes, or until the carrot is tender.

HELPFUL HINT

You can use either green or yellow split peas for this soup – there is no difference in flavour. For a quicker option, use red split lentils as they are quick to cook and do not need pre-soaking.

Meanwhile, place the bacon in a nonstick frying pan and cook over a gentle heat until the bacon is crisp. Remove and drain on absorbent kitchen paper. Season the soup with salt and pepper to taste, then stir in the parsley and milk or cream. Reheat for 2–3 minutes, then ladle into soup bowls. Sprinkle with the bacon and serve immediately with warm garlic bread.

This soup keeps well so why not double up and make enough for 2–3 days. Keep covered in the refrigerator. It is not so suitable for freezing. When reheating, make sure that the soup is brought to the boil then simmered for at least 10 minutes – it needs to be piping hot before eating.

Creamy Caribbean Chicken & Coconut Soup

MAKES 1 PORTION

2 spring onions
1 garlic clove
1 red chilli
50 g/2 oz cooked chicken, shredded or diced
2 tsp vegetable oil
½ tsp ground turmeric

85 ml/3 fl oz coconut milk
300 ml/½ pint chicken stock
1–2 tbsp small soup pasta or spaghetti, broken into small pieces
2 lemon slices

salt and freshly ground black pepper
1–2 tsp freshly chopped coriander
fresh coriander sprigs to garnish (optional)

Trim the spring onions and thinly slice; peel the garlic and finely chop. Cut off the top from the chilli, slit down the side and remove seeds and membrane, then finely chop and reserve. Remove and discard any skin or bones from the cooked chicken and shred using 2 forks and reserve.

Heat a large wok or medium saucepan, add the oil and, when hot, add the spring onions, garlic and chilli and stir-fry for 2 minutes, or until the onion has softened. Stir in the turmeric and cook for 1 minute.

Blend the coconut milk with the chicken stock until smooth, then pour into the wok or medium saucepan. Add the pasta or spaghetti with the lemon slices and bring to the boil. Simmer, half-covered, for 10–12 minutes, or until the pasta is tender; stir occasionally.

HELPFUL HINT

Be careful handling chillies. Either wear rubber gloves or scrub your hands thoroughly after handling them, using plenty of soap and water. Avoid touching eyes or any other sensitive areas.

Remove the lemon slices from the wok or medium saucepan and add the chicken. Season to taste with salt and pepper and simmer for 2–3 minutes, or until the chicken is heated thoroughly. Stir in the chopped coriander and ladle into heated bowls. Garnish with fresh coriander sprigs, if using, and serve immediately.

This soup will not freeze very well, as it has a tendency to separate. However, it will keep fine overnight. Put any unused soup into a bowl, cover with clingfilm and store. Reheat gently.

Chinese Leaf & Mushroom Soup

MAKES 1 PORTION

125 g/4 oz Chinese leaves
10 g/¼ oz dried Chinese
  (shiitake) mushrooms
1 tsp vegetable oil
3 rashers smoked streaky
  bacon, diced

1.25 cm/½ inch piece fresh
  root ginger, peeled
  and finely chopped
50 g/2 oz chestnut
  mushrooms, thinly sliced
300 ml/½ pint chicken stock
2 spring onions, trimmed

and cut into short lengths
1 tsp dry sherry or white
  wine vinegar (optional)
salt and freshly ground
  black pepper
sesame oil for drizzling
  (optional)

Trim the stem ends of the Chinese leaves and cut in half lengthways. Remove the triangular core with a knife, then cut into 2.5 cm/1 inch slices and reserve.

Place the dried Chinese mushrooms in a bowl and pour over enough almost boiling water to cover. Leave to stand for 20 minutes to soften, then gently lift out and squeeze out the liquid. Discard the stems and thinly slice the caps and reserve. Strain the liquid through a muslin-lined sieve or a coffee filter paper and reserve.

Heat a wok or medium saucepan over a medium-high heat, add the oil and, when hot, add the bacon. Stir-fry for 3–4 minutes until crisp and golden, stirring frequently. Add the ginger and chestnut mushrooms and stir-fry for a further 2–3 minutes. Add the chicken stock and bring to the boil, skimming any fat and scum that rises to the surface. Add the spring onions, dry sherry or white wine vinegar, if using, Chinese leaves and Chinese mushrooms and season to taste with salt and pepper. Pour in the reserved soaking liquid and reduce the heat to the lowest possible setting. Simmer gently, covered, until all the vegetables are very tender; this will take about 10 minutes. Add a little water if the liquid has reduced too much. Spoon into soup bowl and drizzle with a little sesame oil, if using. Serve immediately.

TASTY TIP

If Chinese leaves
are not available, use
Savoy cabbage.

This soup will not store well due to the Chinese leaves, which will become very soft and slimy.

Chinese Chicken Soup

MAKES 1 PORTION

50 g/2 oz cooked chicken
1 tsp groundnut or olive oil
2 spring onions, trimmed
   and diagonally sliced
½–1 red chilli, deseeded and
   finely chopped
1 garlic clove, peeled
   and crushed

1.25 cm/½ inch piece root
   ginger, peeled and
   finely grated
450 ml/¾ pint chicken stock
50 g/2 oz medium
   egg noodles
1 small carrot, peeled and
   cut into matchsticks

25 g/1 oz beansprouts
2 tsp soy sauce
1 tsp fish sauce (optional)
fresh coriander leaves, to
   garnish (optional)

TASTY TIP

For a change, replace the chicken with some flaked fish, such as fresh haddock or salmon. Look out for salmon pieces, which are cheaper, or salmon that is on special offer.

TASTY TIP

Increase the vegetable content by adding 25 g/1 oz each of water chestnuts and bamboo shoots and 50 g/2 oz of sugar snap peas and baby corn when you add the chicken.

Remove any skin or bones from the chicken. Place on a chopping board and use two forks to tear the chicken into fine shreds.

Heat the oil in a medium saucepan and fry the spring onions and chilli for 1 minute. Add the garlic and ginger and cook for another minute.

Stir in the chicken stock and gradually bring the mixture to the boil.

Break up the noodles a little and add to the boiling stock with the carrot.

Stir to mix, then reduce the heat to a simmer and cook for 3–4 minutes.

Add the shredded chicken, beansprouts, soy sauce and fish sauce, if using, and stir.

Cook for a further 2–3 minutes until piping hot. Ladle the soup into bowls and sprinkle with the coriander leaves, if using. Serve immediately.

This soup will not keep that well, so eat up!

Winter Hotchpot

MAKES 1 PORTION

small piece gammon, about 125 g/4 oz, or use bacon rashers
1 tsp olive oil
1 small onion, peeled and finely chopped
1 garlic clove, peeled and finely chopped

1 medium carrot, peeled and finely chopped
1 celery stalk, trimmed and finely sliced
1 leek, trimmed and finely sliced
450 ml/¾ pint ham or vegetable stock

25 g/1 oz pearl barley, rinsed
freshly ground black pepper
crusty bread, to serve

Remove any rind and fat from the gammon or bacon rashers and cut into small pieces.

Heat the oil in a medium saucepan over a medium heat and add all the prepared vegetables and gammon or bacon. Cook, stirring occasionally, for 5–8 minutes until the vegetables have softened.

Pour in the stock and bring to the boil. Cover with a lid and simmer for 10 minutes. Add the pearl barley to the pan.

Continue to simmer, covered, for 15–20 minutes until the vegetables and gammon are tender. Add freshly ground black pepper to taste, then serve with crusty bread.

This soup will not freeze well but any remaining soup will keep in the fridge in a clean bowl covered with clingfilm for up to 2 days. Thin down with extra stock or water if too thick after keeping.

Smaller Meals
& Sides

Chinese Fried Rice

MAKES 1 PORTION

125 g/4 oz long-grain rice
2 tsp groundnut or
    vegetable oil
1–2 bacon rashers, chopped
1 garlic clove, peeled and
    finely chopped
1 tsp freshly grated
    root ginger

1 tbsp frozen peas,
    thawed
1 medium egg, beaten
25 g/1 oz beansprouts
salt and freshly ground
    black pepper

To garnish:
1 tbsp roasted peanuts,
    chopped
1 spring onion, trimmed
    and finely chopped

Wash the rice in several changes of water until it runs relatively clear. Drain well. Put into a saucepan or flameproof casserole dish with a tight-fitting lid. Pour in enough water to cover the rice by about 1 cm/½ inch. Add salt and bring to the boil. As soon as the water boils, cover the saucepan, reduce the heat as low as possible and cook for 10 minutes. Remove from the heat and leave to stand for a further 10 minutes. Do not lift the lid while cooking. Leave until cold, and then stir with a fork.

Heat a wok or frying pan, add the oil and, when hot, add the chopped bacon. Stir-fry for 1 minute before adding the garlic and ginger, then stir-fry for a further 30 seconds. Add the cooked rice and peas to the wok or frying pan. Stir-fry over a high heat for 5 minutes. Add the egg and the beansprouts and continue to stir-fry for a further 2 minutes until the egg has set. Season to taste with salt and pepper. Spoon the mixture onto a serving plate and garnish with the peanuts and spring onions. Serve hot or cold.

Spoon any remaining rice into a bowl, cover with clingfilm and store in the refrigerator for the next day. If reheating, ensure that the rice is piping hot before eating. Delicious eaten cold with an omelette. I would not recommend freezing this dish.

TASTY TIP

This dish is an excellent accompaniment to plain grilled chicken or fish or to serve with any meat that has been marinated with Chinese flavours.

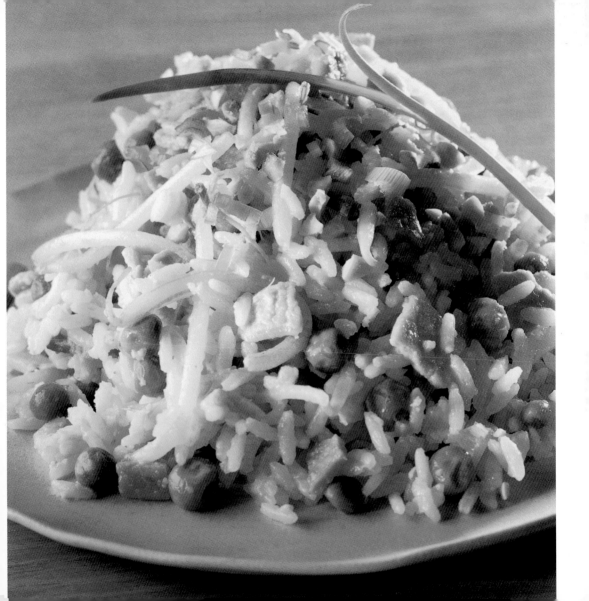

Mediterranean Feast

MAKES 2 PORTIONS

3–4 lettuce leaves such
   as round or cos
50 g/2 oz French beans
75 g/3 oz baby new
   potatoes, scrubbed
2 medium eggs
1 small green pepper
1 small onion, peeled
125 g/4 oz canned tuna in
   brine, drained and flaked
   into small pieces

1–2 tbsp low-fat hard
   cheese, such as Edam,
   cut into small cubes
8 ripe but firm cherry
   tomatoes, quartered
25 g/1 oz black pitted olives,
   halved (optional)
freshly chopped basil,
   to garnish

For the vinaigrette:
2 tbsp light olive or
   vegetable oil
1 tbsp white wine vinegar
1 tbsp lemon juice
1 tbsp grated lemon zest
1 tsp Dijon mustard
1 tsp caster sugar, or to taste
salt and freshly ground
   black pepper

HELPFUL HINT

When buying canned tuna look for ethical line-caught tuna. If you cannot find small cans, store any leftover in a small bowl with the liquid from the can, covered with clingfilm. Eat the next day.

Tear the lettuce into bite-sized pieces and arrange on a serving platter or two individual plates. Cook the French beans in boiling salted water for 8 minutes and the potatoes for 10 minutes or until tender. Drain and rinse in cold water until cool, then cut both the beans and potatoes in half with a sharp knife. Boil the eggs for 10 minutes, then rinse thoroughly under a cold running tap until cool. Remove the shells under water and cut each egg into 4. Remove the seeds from the pepper and cut into thin strips and finely chop the onion. Arrange the beans, potatoes, eggs, peppers and onion on top of the lettuce. Add the tuna, cheese and tomatoes. Sprinkle over the olives, if using, and garnish with the basil.

To make the vinaigrette, place all the ingredients in a screw-topped jar and shake vigorously until everything is mixed thoroughly. Spoon 2 tablespoons over the top of the prepared salad and serve the remainder separately.

If wishing to share this meal with a friend or to keep some for the next day, do not pour the dressing over but serve separately. Store the salad in a bowl, covered with clingfilm in the refrigerator.

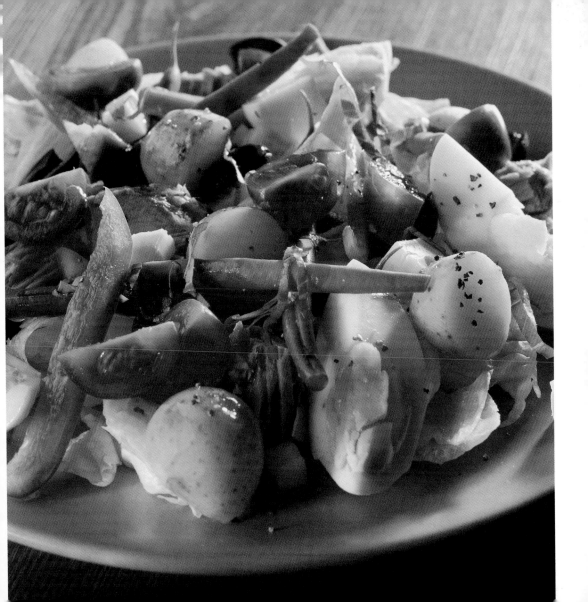

Crispy Baked Potatoes with Ham

MAKES 4 PORTIONS

4 large baking potatoes
4 tsp milk
salt and freshly ground
    black pepper
50 g/2 oz ham, with

fat removed
50 g/2 oz cooked baby broad
    beans, or extra peas
50 g/2 oz cooked
    carrots, diced

50 g/2 oz cooked peas
50 g/2 oz low-fat hard
    cheese such as Edam
    or Cheddar, grated
fresh green salad, to serve

Preheat the oven to 200°C/400°F/Gas Mark 6. Scrub the potatoes dry. Prick with a fork and place on a baking sheet. Cook for 1–1½ hours or until tender when squeezed. (Use oven gloves or a kitchen towel to pick up the potatoes as they will be very hot.) Cut the potatoes in half horizontally and scoop out all the flesh into a bowl. Pour the milk into the bowl and mix thoroughly with the potatoes. Season to taste with salt and pepper. Cut the ham into strips and carefully stir into the potato mixture with the broad beans, if using, and carrots and peas.

Pile the mixture back into the potato shells and sprinkle grated cheese on the top. Place under a hot grill and cook until golden and heated through. Serve immediately with a fresh green salad.

These stuffed potatoes will keep well in the refrigerator for 2–3 days, but if planning to do so make up the recipe as above then only grill what you will eat that day. Place the remaining potatoes on a plate and cover with clingfilm. Keep in the refrigerator until required. When ready to eat, preheat the oven to 200°C/400°C/Gas Mark 6 and cook the potatoes on a baking sheet for 30 minutes or until piping hot.

Alternatively, you can use a microwave (which uses less energy and is quicker than an oven): cook the raw potatoes in the microwave allowing 4–6 minutes for each potato. Finish as per the recipe. To reheat, place the potatoes on a plate, cover with clingfilm and pierce a couple of times, then heat on High for 1 minute for each potato. If liked, place under a preheated grill for 2 minutes to crisp the top. Allow to stand for 1 minute before eating.

Sweetcorn Fritters

MAKES 2 PORTIONS

3 tbsp vegetable oil
1 small onion, peeled
   and finely chopped
½–1 red chilli, deseeded
   and finely chopped
1 garlic clove, peeled
   and crushed
½ tsp ground coriander

175 g/6 oz canned or thawed
   frozen sweetcorn
2 spring onions, trimmed
   and finely sliced
1 egg, lightly beaten
salt and freshly ground
   black pepper
1–2 tbsp plain flour

½ tsp baking powder
spring onion curls, to
   garnish (optional)
Thai-style chutney,
   to serve

HELPFUL HINT

When using chilli, remember that it is not only the seeds that contain the heat, it is also the membrane (the skin to which the seeds are attached) so if a mild flavour is preferred, remove both.

Heat 1 tablespoon of the oil in a frying pan, add the onion and cook gently for 7–8 minutes or until beginning to soften. Add the chilli, garlic and ground coriander and cook for 1 minute, stirring continuously. Remove from the heat.

Drain the sweetcorn and tip into a mixing bowl. Lightly mash with a potato masher to break down the corn a little. Add the cooked onion mixture to the bowl with the spring onions and beaten egg. Season to taste with salt and pepper, and then stir to mix together. Sift the flour and baking powder over the mixture and stir in. Heat 2 tablespoons of the oil in a large frying pan. Drop 4 or 5 heaped teaspoonfuls of the sweetcorn mixture into the pan, and using a fish slice or spatula, flatten each to make a 1 cm/½ inch thick fritter. Fry the fritters for 3 minutes, or until golden brown on the underside, turn over and fry for a further 3 minutes, or until cooked through and crisp. Remove the fritters from the pan and drain on absorbent kitchen paper. Keep warm while cooking the remaining fritters, adding a little more oil if needed. Garnish with spring onion curls, if using, and serve immediately with a Thai-style chutney.

If any fritters remain uneaten, store on a plate lightly covered in the refrigerator overnight. Fry in a little oil on both sides to reheat. Take care not to burn but ensure that the fritters are piping hot. Drain on kitchen paper to absorb any excess oil.

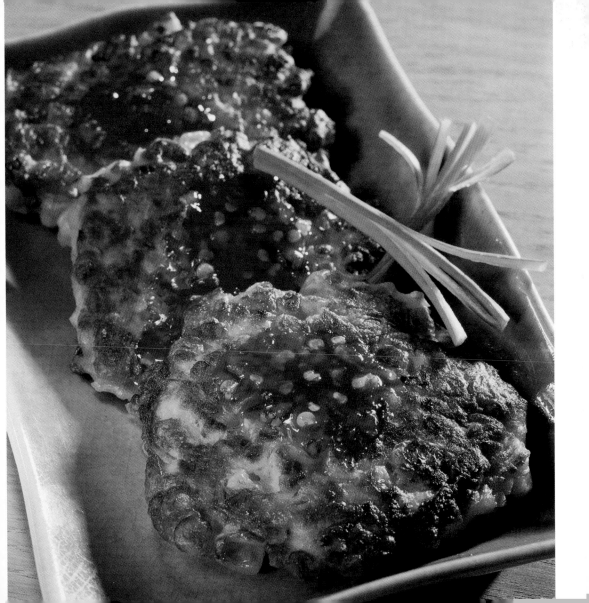

Spanish Omelette with Fish

MAKES 1 PORTION

2 tbsp sunflower oil
125 g/4 oz potatoes,
    peeled and cut into
    1 cm/½ inch cubes
1 small onion, peeled
    and cut into wedges
1 large garlic clove,
    peeled and thinly sliced
1 small red pepper,
    deseeded, quartered
    and thinly sliced

50 g/2 oz fresh white fish
    such as coley or whiting
salt and freshly ground
    black pepper
1 tbsp butter or
    margarine, melted
1 tbsp milk
2 medium eggs, beaten
2 tsp freshly chopped
    flat-leaf parsley

2 tbsp mature Cheddar
    cheese, grated

To serve:
crusty bread
tossed green salad, to serve

TASTY TIP

One of the good things about Spanish Omelettes is that they are often served cold cut into small squares or wedges. So any left over can be eaten the next day cold. Super for a quick lunch.

HELPFUL HINT

When buying fresh fish look for the cheaper fish: coley, whiting, dab and fresh haddock. As an alternative to fresh, use canned, such as tuna, sardines, sild or mackerel. Remember to drain first.

Heat the oil in a medium nonstick heavy-based frying pan, add the potatoes, onion and garlic and cook gently for 10–15 minutes until golden brown, then add the red pepper and cook for 3 minutes.

Discard any skin or small bones from the fish. Cut into small pieces. Place into a bowl, toss in the melted butter or margarine with the milk and add seasoning. Reserve.

When the vegetables are cooked, drain off any excess oil and stir in the beaten egg with the chopped parsley. Pour the fish mixture over the top and cook gently for 5 minutes, or until the eggs become firm.

Sprinkle the grated cheese over the top and place the pan under a preheated hot grill. Cook for 2–3 minutes until the cheese is golden and bubbling. Carefully slide the omelette onto a large plate and serve immediately with plenty of bread and salad.

Chicken Wraps

MAKES 2 PORTIONS

For the stir-fried chicken:
2 skinless chicken
    breast fillets
finely grated zest and
    juice of 1 lemon
2 tsp sugar
1–2 tsp dried oregano
½ tsp ground cinnamon

¼ tsp cayenne pepper
    or to taste
1½ tbsp sunflower oil
1 small onion, peeled and
    sliced
1 small green, red and
    yellow pepper,
    deseeded and sliced

salt and freshly ground
    black pepper

To serve:
flour tortillas
sour cream
guacamole

HELPFUL HINT

It is very important that chicken is thoroughly cooked. To test if cooked, pierce the thickest part and if it feels tender and the juices running out are clear and not pink then the chicken is cooked.

TASTY TIP

Replace the chicken with a mixture of vegetables such as peppers, onion, broccoli, leek and courgette, then sprinkle with peanuts to serve. Or use a small piece of fish such as whiting or coley. Cook as for chicken.

Slice the chicken across the grain into strips. Place in a bowl with the lemon zest and juice, sugar, oregano, cinnamon and cayenne pepper. Mix well and leave to marinate in the refrigerator for at least 30 minutes or longer if time permits.

Heat ½ tablespoon of the oil in a wok or frying pan and stir-fry the onion for 5 minutes until lightly coloured. Remove with a slotted spoon and reserve.

When ready to eat, heat 2–4 tortillas as directed on the packet. Keep warm.

Add the remaining oil to the wok or frying pan and heat. Drain the chicken from the marinade and add it to pan. Cook for 8 minutes, then return the onions, add the pepper slices and cook for a further 4–5 minutes, or until the chicken is cooked through and the vegetables are tender. Season to taste with salt and pepper and serve immediately with the warm tortillas, sour cream and guacamole.

Any remaining chicken and vegetable mix will keep well in the refrigerator. Once cool, place on a plate, cover with clingfilm and keep overnight in the refrigerator. Next day use cold in a warm tortilla.

Gingered Fish Steaks

MAKES 1 PORTION

1.25 cm /½ inch piece fresh
  root ginger, peeled
2 spring onions
1 tsp freshly
  chopped parsley

1 tsp soft brown sugar
1 x 175 g /6 oz thick white
  fish steak such as coley,
  fresh haddock or pollack

salt and freshly ground
  black pepper
2 tsp butter or margarine
freshly cooked vegetables,
  to serve

Preheat the grill and line the grill rack with a layer of kitchen foil. Coarsely grate the piece of ginger. Trim the spring onions and cut into thin strips.

Mix the spring onions, ginger, chopped parsley and sugar. Add 1 tablespoon of water.

Wipe the fish steak. Season to taste with salt and pepper. Place on to a 20.5 x 20.5 cm/8 x 8 inch foil square.

Carefully spoon the spring onions and ginger mixture over the fish.

Cut the butter or margarine into small cubes and place over the fish.

Loosely fold the foil over the steaks to enclose the fish and to make a parcel.

Place under the preheated grill and cook for 10–12 minutes or until cooked and the flesh has turned opaque.

Serve immediately with the freshly cooked vegetables.

HELPFUL HINT

When buying fresh fish take care that it is really fresh. If it smells 'fishy', avoid, as white fish should not have a strong smell. It should be refrigerated as soon as possible once bought and used within 2 days.

Turkey Hash with Potato & Beetroot

MAKES 1 PORTION

2 tsp vegetable oil
15 g/½ oz butter or
  margarine
1 rasher streaky bacon,
  diced or sliced
1 small onion, peeled
  and finely chopped

125 g/4 oz cooked
  turkey, diced
125 g/4 oz finely chopped
  cooked potatoes
1 tsp freshly
  chopped parsley
2 tsp plain flour

75g/3 oz cooked
  beetroot, diced
green salad,
  to serve

In a small heavy-based frying pan, heat the oil and half the butter or margarine over a medium heat until sizzling. Add the bacon and cook for 2 minutes, or until crisp and golden, stirring occasionally. Using a slotted spoon, transfer to a bowl. Add the onion to the pan and cook for 3–4 minutes, or until soft and golden, stirring frequently.

Meanwhile, add the turkey, potatoes, parsley and flour to the cooked bacon in the bowl. Stir and toss gently, then fold in the diced beetroot.

Add half the remaining butter or margarine to the frying pan and then the turkey vegetable mixture. Stir, then spread the mixture to evenly cover the bottom of the frying pan. Cook over a medium heat for 15 minutes, or until the underside is crisp and brown, pressing the hash firmly into a cake with a spatula. Remove from the heat.

Invert a large plate over the frying pan and, holding the plate and frying pan together with an oven glove, turn the hash out onto the plate. Heat the remaining butter or margarine in the pan, slide the hash back into the pan and cook for 4 minutes, or until crisp and brown on the other side. Invert onto the plate again and serve immediately with a green salad.

USEFUL TIP

Vacuum-packed beetroot needs to be kept in the fridge once opened and used within 2–3 days. If in a jar it is normally preserved in vinegar and once opened will keep in the fridge for 1–2 weeks.

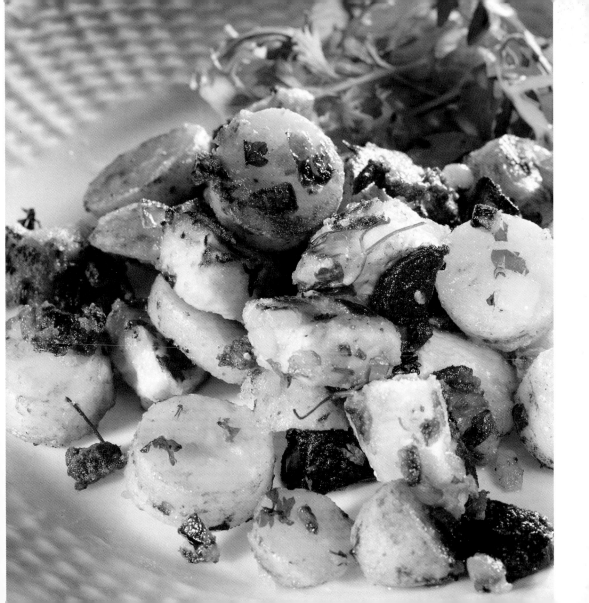

Huevos Rancheros

MAKES 1 PORTION

2 tsp olive or vegetable oil
1 small onion, peeled and
  finely chopped
½ small red pepper, deseeded
  and finely chopped
1 garlic clove, peeled and
  finely chopped
1–2 green chillies, deseeded
  and finely chopped,
  and/or ½ tsp chilli powder

½ tsp ground cumin
½ tsp ground coriander
1 tsp freshly
  chopped coriander
2 medium-sized ripe plum
  tomatoes, peeled,
  deseeded and
  roughly chopped
¼ tsp sugar
2 small eggs

2 flour tortillas
salt and freshly ground
  black pepper
sprigs of fresh coriander,
  to garnish
refried beans, to serve
  (optional)

HELPFUL HINT

Whether you use fresh chillies and/or chilli powder depends on your heat tolerance. When using fresh chillies it is worth remembering that as a general rule the smaller the chilli, the hotter it is.

Heat the oil in a medium heavy-based saucepan. Add the onion and pepper and cook over a medium heat for 10 minutes. Add the garlic, chillies and/or chilli powder, ground cumin and ground and chopped coriander and cook for a further minute. Add the tomatoes and sugar. Stir well, cover and cook gently for 10 minutes. Uncover and cook for a further 8–10 minutes.

Lightly poach the eggs in a small frying pan, filled with gently simmering water. Drain well and keep warm.

Place the tortillas briefly under a preheated hot grill. Turn once and remove from the grill when hot.

Season the tomato sauce to taste with salt and pepper. To serve, arrange the tortillas on a serving plate, top with the two eggs and spoon the sauce over. Garnish with sprigs of fresh coriander and serve immediately with warmed refried beans, if liked.

The tomato sauce will keep well in the refrigerator. Spoon into a small bowl and cover with clingfilm. Use within 2–3 days.

Warm Potato, Pear & Pecan Salad

MAKES 1 PORTION

125 g/4 oz new potatoes, preferably red-skinned, unpeeled
1 tsp Dijon or English mustard, or to taste
2 tsp white wine vinegar

or use lemon juice
2 tbsp groundnut or vegetable oil
½ tsp poppy seeds
salt and freshly ground black pepper

1 firm ripe dessert pear
2 tsp lemon juice
25 g/1 oz baby spinach leaves or cos lettuce
25 g/1 oz toasted pecan nuts or walnuts

Scrub the potatoes, then cook in a saucepan of lightly salted boiling water for 15 minutes, or until tender. Drain, cut into halves, or quarters if large, and place in a serving bowl.

In a small bowl or jug, whisk together the mustard and vinegar or lemon juice if using. Gradually add the oil until the mixture begins to thicken. Stir in the poppy seeds and season to taste with salt and pepper.

Pour half the dressing over the hot potatoes and toss gently to coat. Leave until the potatoes have soaked up the dressing and are just warm.

Meanwhile, quarter and core the pear. Cut into thin slices, then sprinkle with the two teaspoons of lemon juice to prevent them from going brown. Add to the potatoes with the spinach or lettuce leaves and toasted pecan nuts or walnuts. Gently mix together.

Drizzle the remaining dressing over the salad. Serve immediately, before the spinach starts to wilt.

HELPFUL HINT

To toast the nuts, bake in a single layer in a preheated oven at 180°C/350°F/Gas Mark 4 for 5 minutes, or under a medium grill for 3–4 minutes, turning frequently. Be careful – they burn easily.

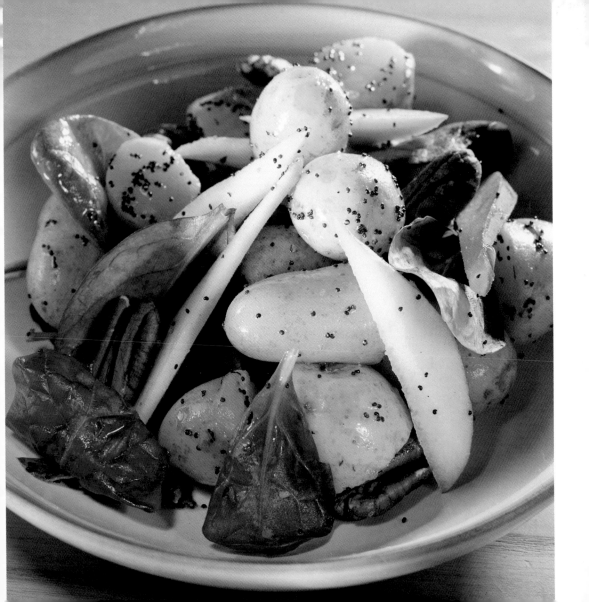

Three Tomato Pizza

MAKES 2 PIZZAS

2 bought pizza bases

For the topping:
3 plum tomatoes
8 cherry tomatoes

6 sun-dried tomatoes or extra
    plum or cherry tomatoes
pinch sea salt
1 tbsp freshly chopped basil
2 tbsp olive or sunflower oil

125 g/4 oz mozzarella
    cheese, sliced
freshly ground black pepper
fresh basil leaves, to garnish

Preheat the oven to 220°C/425°F/Gas Mark 7. Place one or two baking sheets in the oven to heat. Place the 2 pizza bases on the work surface and reserve.

Slice the plum tomatoes, halve the cherry tomatoes and chop the sun-dried tomatoes, if using, into small pieces. Arrange the tomatoes on top of the two pizza bases and season to taste with the sea salt.

Sprinkle with the chopped basil and drizzle with the oil. Top with the mozzarella slices and season with black pepper.

Transfer onto the heated baking sheets and cook for 20–25 minutes, or until the cheese is golden brown and bubbling. If necessary, switch the trays so that they are both ready at the same time. Remove from the oven, garnish with the basil and serve.

TASTY TIP

Other ingredients can be added to the pizza. Try thinly sliced yellow pepper, or an onion, peeled and thinly sliced. Or try thinly sliced salami or flaked tuna.

The cooked pizzas will keep overnight in the refrigerator or will freeze. To freeze, cut the cooked pizza into portions, place uncovered on a clean baking sheet and then place in the freezer and leave for 2–3 hours until frozen. Once frozen, place in freezer bags and keep no longer than 2–3 weeks. Portions can then be thawed within 1½–2 hours and reheated under a medium grill.

Nutty Stuffed Onions

MAKES 1–2 PORTIONS

2 medium onions, peeled
1 small garlic cloves,
   peeled and crushed
2 tbsp brown or white
   breadcrumbs
1 tbsp sultanas or raisins

1 tbsp pine or other
   nuts, chopped
1 tbsp hard cheese,
   such as Edam, grated
1 tsp freshly chopped
   parsley

salt and freshly ground
   black pepper
1 small egg yolk, beaten
salad leaves,
   to serve

Preheat the oven to 200°C/400°F/Gas Mark 6. Bring a pan of water to the boil, add the onions and cook gently for about 15 minutes. Drain well. Allow the onions to cool, then slice in half horizontally. Scoop out most of the onion flesh but leave a reasonably firm shell.

Chop up 2 tablespoons of the onion flesh and place in a bowl with the crushed garlic, most of the breadcrumbs (reserving some for sprinkling), sultanas or raisins, pine nuts, grated cheese and parsley. Season to taste with salt and pepper.

Mix the breadcrumb mixture together thoroughly. Bind together with as much of the beaten egg as necessary to make a firm filling.

Pile the mixture back into the onion shells and sprinkle with the remaining breadcrumbs. Place on an oiled baking tray and cook in the preheated oven for 20–30 minutes, or until golden brown. Serve immediately with the salad leaves.

Any remaining stuffed onions can be kept in the refrigerator. Allow to cool, then place on a plate and cover with clingfilm. Keep for up to 2 days. I would not recommend freezing. If wishing to reheat, pierce the clingfilm in 2–3 places. Place in the microwave and heat on High for 2 minutes. Allow to stand for 1 minute; if not piping hot, reheat for an extra minute.

FOOD FACT

While this dish is delicious on its own, it also complements barbecued meat and fish. The onion takes on a mellow, nutty flavour when baked.

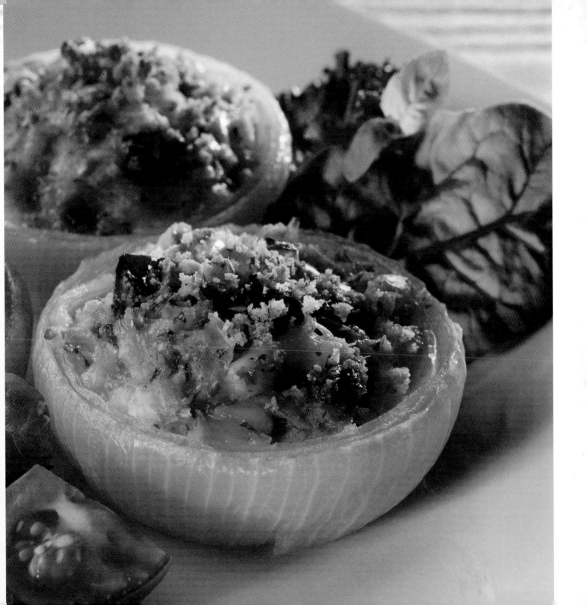

Garlic Mushroom Galettes

MAKES 2

50 g/2 oz piece bought
   puff pastry
1 small onion, peeled
1 red chilli, deseeded
2 garlic cloves, peeled

75 g/3 oz mixed mushrooms
   (e.g. large field, button
   or chestnut)
25 g/1 oz butter
   or margarine
1 tsp freshly chopped parsley

50 g/2 oz mozzarella
   cheese, sliced

To serve:
cherry tomatoes
mixed green salad leaves

Preheat the oven to 220°C/425°F/Gas Mark 7. On a lightly floured surface roll out the pastry very thinly. Cut out two 15 cm/6 inch circles and place on a lightly oiled baking sheet.

Slice the onion thinly, then divide into rings and reserve. Slice the chilli thinly and slice the garlic into wafer-thin slivers. Add to the onions and reserve. Wipe or lightly rinse the mushrooms. Halve or quarter any large mushrooms and keep the small ones whole.

Heat the butter or margarine in a frying pan and fry the onion, chilli and garlic gently for about 3 minutes. Add the mushrooms and cook for about 5 minutes, or until beginning to soften. Stir the parsley into the mushroom mixture and drain off any excess liquid.

Pile the mushroom mixture onto the pastry circles within 5 mm/¼ inch of the edge. Arrange the sliced mozzarella cheese on top. Bake in the preheated oven for 12–15 minutes, or until golden brown and serve with the tomatoes and salad.

If you only want to make 1 galette for now, cook 1 then place the remaining filling in a small bowl, and the spare pastry round on a clean baking tray, cover and store both overnight in the refrigerator. Cook the next evening.

HELPFUL HINT

Fresh puff pastry usually comes in large amounts, so cut into small portions then freeze. Take out and use as required.

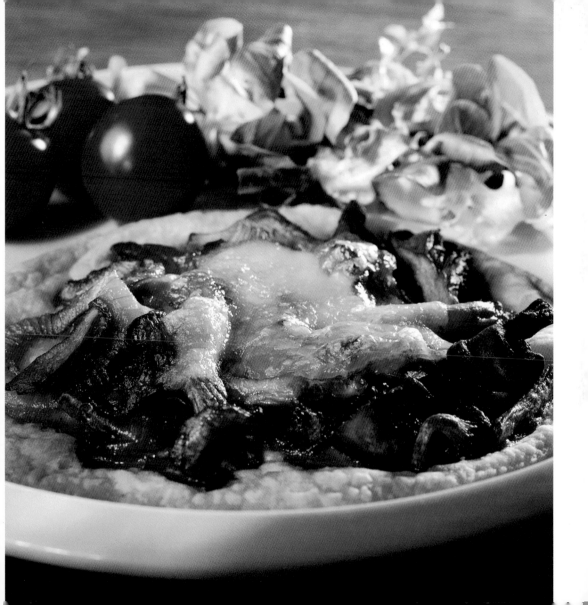

Onion Bhajis

MAKES 10–12

1 large onion, peeled
125 g/4 oz chickpea flour
small piece fresh root
  ginger, peeled and grated
½–1 small chilli, deseeded
  and finely chopped

½ tsp turmeric
½ tsp ground coriander
2 tbsp freshly
  chopped coriander
freshly milled salt,
  to taste

50–85 ml/2–3 fl oz water
vegetable oil,
  for deep-frying

Finely slice the onions and place in a mixing bowl with the flour, spices and coriander. Add salt to taste.

Slowly stir in the water and mix to form a thick consistency. Form into loose balls.

Heat the oil in a deep-fryer or wok to a temperature of 180°C/350°F. Drop the bhajis, about 2 or 3 at a time, into the hot oil and deep-fry for 2–3 minutes, or until golden brown and crisp. Remove with a slotted spoon and drain on absorbent kitchen paper. Serve.

The bhajis will not keep for long, as they quickly become soggy, but they can be stored in the refrigerator overnight on a plate and covered with clingfilm. Do not freeze. They can be reheated in the oven for about 5–8 minutes or refried in some hot oil. This will make them crisp.

TASTY TIP

Other ingredients can be used as well – try thinly sliced assorted peppers, courgette, very thinly sliced carrot or even shredded white cabbage.

Cheesy Chicken Burgers

MAKES 2 SMALL BURGERS

1 tbsp sunflower oil
1 small onion, peeled
and finely chopped
1 garlic clove, peeled
and crushed
¼ red pepper, deseeded
and finely chopped
175 g/6 oz fresh chicken mince
1 tbsp 0%-fat Greek yogurt
2 tbsp fresh brown or white
breadcrumbs

1 tsp freshly chopped herbs,
such as parsley or tarragon
15 g/½ oz Cheshire cheese,
crumbled
salt and freshly ground
black pepper

**For the sweetcorn and
carrot relish (optional):**
50 g/2 oz canned
sweetcorn, drained

1 small carrot, peeled, grated
½ green chilli, deseeded and
finely chopped
1 tsp vinegar or lemon juice
1 tsp light soft brown sugar

To serve:
wholemeal or granary rolls
lettuce
sliced tomatoes
mixed salad leaves

Heat the oil in a frying pan and gently cook the onion and garlic for 5 minutes. Add the red pepper and cook for 5 minutes. Transfer into a bowl. Add the chicken, yogurt, breadcrumbs, herbs and cheese and season to taste with salt and pepper. Mix well. Divide the mixture equally into 2 and shape into burgers. Cover and chill for at least 20 minutes.

Put all the relish ingredients in a small saucepan with 1 tablespoon water and heat gently, stirring occasionally until all the sugar has dissolved. Cover and cook over a low heat for 2 minutes, then uncover and cook for a further minute, or until the relish is thick.

Preheat the grill to medium. Place the burgers on a lightly oiled grill pan and grill for 8–10 minutes on each side, or until browned and completely cooked through. Warm the rolls if liked, then split and fill with the burgers, lettuce, tomatoes and relish. Serve immediately with the salad leaves.

Prepared but uncooked burgers can be refrigerated for up to 2 days on a clean plate covered with clingfilm. Or, providing that the mince has not been previously frozen, open freeze on a plate for 3–4 hours until solid, wrap in kitchen foil, label and date. Thaw overnight in the fridge.

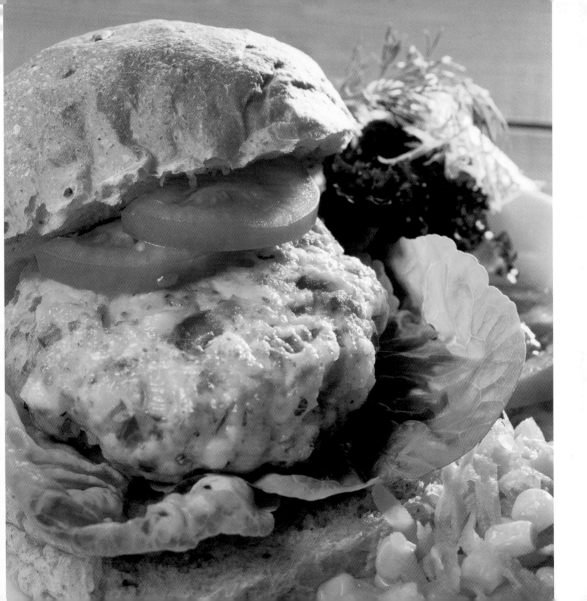

Spanish Baked Tomatoes

MAKES 1–2 PORTIONS

50 g/2 oz whole-grain rice
300 ml/½ pint
vegetable stock
2 tsp sunflower oil
1 shallot, peeled and
finely chopped
1 garlic clove, peeled
and crushed

½ green pepper, deseeded
and cut into small dice
½–1 red chilli, deseeded and
finely chopped
25 g/1 oz button mushrooms
finely chopped
1 tsp freshly
chopped oregano

salt and freshly ground
black pepper
2 large ripe beef tomatoes
1 small egg, beaten
1 tsp caster sugar
basil leaves, to garnish
crusty bread, to serve

Preheat the oven to 180°C/350°F/Gas Mark 4. Place the rice in a saucepan, pour over the vegetable stock and bring to the boil. Simmer for 30 minutes or until the rice is tender. Drain and turn into a mixing bowl.

Add 1 teaspoon of sunflower oil to a small nonstick pan and gently fry the shallot, garlic, pepper, chilli and mushrooms for 2 minutes. Add to the rice with the chopped oregano. Season with plenty of salt and pepper.

Slice the top off each tomato and reserve. Scoop out the flesh, removing the hard core. Pass the flesh through a sieve. Add 1 tablespoon of the juice to the rice mixture. Stir in the beaten egg and mix. Sprinkle a little sugar in the base of each tomato. Pile the rice mixture into the shells. Place the tomatoes in a baking dish and pour a little cold water around them. Replace their lids and drizzle a few drops of sunflower oil over the tops. Bake for about 25 minutes. Garnish with the basil leaves, season with black pepper and serve immediately with crusty bread.

If liked, keep one tomato for the next day: place on a plate, cover with clingfilm and refrigerate. It would be better to prepare the tomato but not to bake it until needed. Reheat cooked tomatoes in the microwave. Recover with clean clingfilm and pierce 2–3 times. Heat on High for 2 minutes, allow to stand for 1 minute. Check it is piping hot; if not, heat for a further minute.

TASTY TIP

This dish is also delicious made with meat. Heat the frying pan and dry-fry 50 g/2 oz minced beef on a high heat until cooked through and brown, before adding the rest of the ingredients.

Roasted Mixed Vegetables with Garlic & Herb Sauce

MAKES 2 PORTIONS

3–4 large garlic cloves
1 medium onion, peeled
  and cut into wedges
2 carrots, peeled
  and quartered
1 parsnip, peeled

3 small potatoes, scrubbed
  and halved
2 fresh rosemary sprigs
2 fresh thyme sprigs
2 tbsp olive or vegetable oil
salt and freshly ground
  black pepper

75 g/3 oz low-fat soft cheese
  with herbs and garlic
2 tbsp milk
zest of ½ lemon
thyme sprigs, to garnish

Preheat the oven to 220°C/425°F/Gas Mark 7. Cut the garlic cloves in half horizontally. Put into a large roasting tin with all the vegetables and herbs. Add the oil, season well with salt and pepper and toss together to coat lightly in the oil. Cover with kitchen foil and roast in the preheated oven for 30 minutes. Remove the kitchen foil and cook for a further 15 minutes or until all the vegetables are tender and slightly charred. Remove the tin from the oven and allow to cool.

In a small saucepan, melt the low-fat soft cheese together with the milk and lemon zest.

Remove the garlic from the roasting tin and squeeze the flesh into a bowl. Mash thoroughly then add to the sauce. Heat through gently. Season the vegetables to taste. Pour some sauce into a small ramekin and garnish with thyme sprigs. Serve immediately with the roasted vegetables and the sauce to dip.

This will not freeze well but will keep overnight in the refrigerator. Reheat gently either in the microwave on High for 1–2 minutes or in a saucepan on the hob, stirring frequently. Pour the sauce over to reheat.

TASTY TIP

This dish can also be served as a side to grilled or roasted fish or chicken. Marinade or drizzle the fish with a little olive oil, lemon juice and zest, and mixed herbs.

Easy-peasy Pasta

Baked Macaroni Cheese

MAKES 4 PORTIONS

350 g/12 oz macaroni
50 g/2 oz butter or
   margarine
1 onion, peeled and
   finely chopped
40 g/1½ oz plain flour
600 ml/1 pt milk
1–2 dried or fresh bay leaves

salt and freshly ground
   black pepper
freshly grated nutmeg
   (optional)
1 tbsp Dijon or English
   mustard
125 g/4 oz mature
   Cheddar cheese, grated

1 tbsp dried breadcrumbs
   (optional)
1 tbsp freshly grated
   Parmesan cheese
   (optional)
basil sprig, to garnish
   (optional)

Preheat the oven to 190°C/375°F/Gas Mark 5, 10 minutes before cooking. Bring a large pan of lightly salted water to a rolling boil. Add the macaroni and cook according to the packet instructions, or until *al dente*. Drain thoroughly and reserve.

Meanwhile, melt the butter or margarine in a large, heavy-based saucepan, add the onion and cook, stirring frequently, for 5–7 minutes, until softened. Sprinkle in the flour and cook, stirring constantly, for 2 minutes. Remove from the heat, stir in the milk, return to the heat and cook, stirring, until a smooth sauce has formed. Add the bay leaf(ves) and season to taste with salt and pepper and nutmeg, if using. Simmer for about 5 minutes, stirring frequently. Remove from the heat, add the mustard and Cheddar cheese and stir until the cheese has melted. Stir in the macaroni then tip into a lightly oiled ovenproof dish. If using the breadcrumbs and Parmesan cheese, sprinkle over the macaroni. Bake in the preheated oven for 30–35 minutes until golden. Garnish with a basil sprig, if using, and serve immediately, removing the bay leaf(ves).

Spoon any uneaten portions into small dishes. Store in the refrigerator covered with clingfilm and use within 3 days. Reheat in a saucepan, adding a little more milk to thin down the sauce. Alternatively, wrap, label, date and freeze the dishes. Use within 1 month. Once thawed, reheat as above adding a little milk. Adjust seasoning, as freezing can alter the seasoning.

HELPFUL HINT

Make sure that you only simmer the macaroni until just *al dente* and drain straight away, as it will be further cooked in the oven where it needs to soak up the flavoursome sauce.

Creamy Chicken & Mushroom Macaroni

MAKES 1 LARGE PORTION

125 g/4 oz macaroni
40 g/1½ oz butter or
  margarine
50 g/2 oz button mushrooms,
  wiped and halved
75 g/3 oz cooked chicken,
  skinned and chopped

2 tsp cornflour
300 ml/½ pint
  semi-skimmed milk
50 g/2 oz Cheddar
  cheese, chopped
1 tsp freshly chopped sage
  (optional)

1 tsp freshly chopped
  chives, plus extra chive
  leaves to garnish
  (optional)
salt and freshly ground
  black pepper

Bring a large pan of lightly salted water to a rolling boil. Add the macaroni and cook according to the packet instructions, or until *al dente*.

Meanwhile, melt the butter or margarine in a large frying pan, add the mushrooms and cook for 5 minutes, or until golden, stirring occasionally. Add the chicken to the pan and cook for 2 minutes, stirring occasionally.

Blend the cornflour with a little of the milk in a jug to form a smooth paste, then gradually blend in the remaining milk and pour into the frying pan. Bring to the boil slowly, stirring constantly. Add the cheese and cook for 2 minutes, stirring until melted. Stir in the sage, if using, and chives. Season to taste with salt and pepper. Drain the macaroni thoroughly and return to the pan. Pour the chicken and mushroom sauce over the macaroni and stir lightly to coat. Tip into a warmed serving dish, and serve immediately with extra cheese, if liked.

Keep leftovers overnight in the refrigerator in a clean bowl covered with clingfilm. To reheat, place into a small saucepan and heat on the hob stirring frequently, until piping hot. The microwave could also be used to reheat. Simply pierce the clingfilm 2–3 times then heat on High for 1–2 minutes, remove and stir. Continue to heat for 2 minutes or until the macaroni and chicken are piping hot. Allow to stand for 1 minute. Either way you may need to add a little more milk.

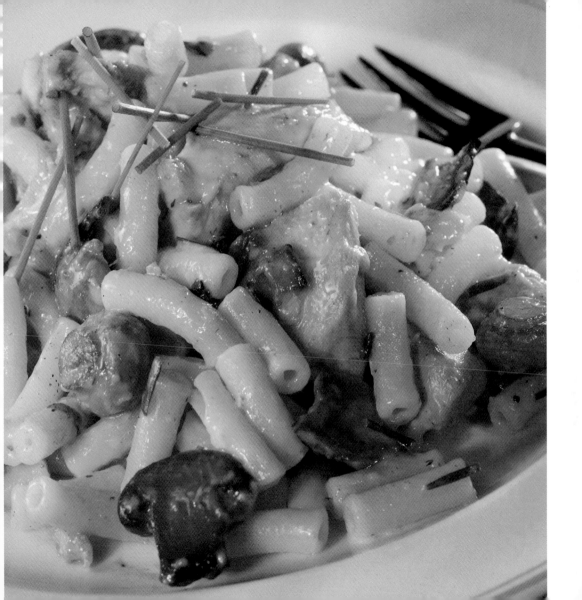

Penne with Mixed Peppers & Garlic

MAKES 1 LARGE PORTION

½ each of green, red and yellow peppers
2 tbsp olive or sunflower oil
1 small onion, peeled and sliced
1 garlic clove, peeled and crushed

2 rashers smoked streaky bacon, finely chopped
150 ml/¼ pint chicken stock
salt and freshly ground black pepper
125 g/4 oz fresh or dried penne

1 tsp freshly chopped parsley
2 tsp Parmesan or Cheddar cheese, finely grated

To serve:
green salad
warm granary bread

Preheat the grill and line the grill rack with kitchen foil. Deseed the peppers and place cut side down on the grill rack. Cook under the grill until the skins become blistered and black all over. Place the peppers in a polythene bag and allow to cool, then discard the skin and slice thinly.

Heat the oil in a heavy-based pan. Add the onion, garlic and bacon and cook for 4–5 minutes, or until the onion has softened. Add the peppers and cook for 1 minute. Pour in the stock and season to taste with salt and pepper. Cover and simmer for 10 minutes.

Meanwhile, bring a large pan of lightly salted water to a rolling boil. Add the penne and cook according to the packet instructions, about 3–4 minutes, or until al dente. Drain thoroughly and return to the pan.

Pour the pepper sauce over the pasta and toss lightly. Tip into a warmed serving dish and sprinkle with the chopped parsley and grated cheese. Serve immediately with a green salad and warm granary bread.

Keep any remaining pasta and sauce in a clean bowl, covered with clingfilm overnight in the refrigerator. The next day reheat on High for 2 minutes in the microwave.

HELPFUL HINT

Grilling brings out all the delicious flavour of peppers. Do make sure that they are blackened and blistered so that the skins simply slip off.

Gnocchetti with Broccoli & Bacon Sauce

MAKES 1 LARGE PORTION

125 g/4 oz broccoli florets
2 tbsp olive or sunflower oil
2 bacon rashers,
   finely chopped
1 small onion, peeled
   and finely chopped

1–2 garlic cloves, peeled
   and sliced
150 ml/¼ pint milk
125 g/4 oz gnocchetti (little
   elongated ribbed shells)
   or farfalle

25 g/1 oz freshly grated
   Parmesan or Cheddar
   cheese, plus extra
   to serve
salt and freshly ground
   black pepper

Bring a large pan of salted water to the boil. Add the broccoli florets and cook for about 8–10 minutes, or until very soft. Drain thoroughly, allow to cool slightly then chop finely and reserve.

Heat the olive or sunflower oil in a heavy-based pan, add the bacon and cook over a medium heat for 5 minutes, or until golden and crisp. Add the onion and cook for a further 5 minutes, or until soft and lightly golden. Add the garlic and cook for 1 minute.

Transfer the chopped broccoli to the bacon mixture and pour in the milk. Bring slowly to the boil and simmer rapidly for about 8–10 minutes, or until reduced to a creamy texture.

Meanwhile, bring a large pan of lightly salted water to a rolling boil. Add the pasta and cook according to the packet instructions, or until *al dente*. Drain the pasta thoroughly, reserving a little of the cooking water. Add the pasta and the cheese to the broccoli mixture. Stir, adding enough of the reserved cooking water to make a creamy sauce. Season to taste with salt and pepper. Serve immediately with extra cheese.

If liked, this recipe can be doubled up in order to keep for a further meal. Make as above simply doubling the ingredients. Spoon into small bowls, cover with clingfilm and store in the refrigerator for 2–3 days. When ready to eat, tip into a small saucepan, add a little extra milk. Heat gently, stirring frequently until piping hot.

FOOD FACT

There are plenty of different pasta shapes that can be used in place of the gnocchetti. Try farfalle (bows), fusilli (small spirals), penne (tube shape) or rigatoni (bigger, ridged tubes).

Fusilli Pasta with Spicy Tomato Salsa

MAKES 1 LARGE PORTION

2 medium ripe tomatoes
1 tbsp lemon juice
 (removed lime)
1 tbsp grated zest of
 1 lemon
1 shallot, peeled and
 finely chopped

1–2 garlic cloves, peeled and
 finely chopped
½–1 red chilli, depending on
 heat tolerance
½–1 green chilli or ½–1 tsp
 dried crushed chillies
125 g/4 oz fresh or dried

fusilli pasta
2 tbsp natural or
 Greek yogurt
2 tsp freshly chopped basil
 (optional)
oregano sprig, to garnish
 (optional)

Place the tomatoes in a bowl and cover with boiling water. Allow to stand until the skins start to peel away. Remove the skins from the tomatoes, divide each tomato in four and remove all the seeds. Chop the flesh into small dice and put in a small pan. Add the lemon juice and zest and stir well. Add the chopped shallot and garlic.

If using the chillies remove the seeds carefully, chop the flesh finely and add to the pan. Or stir in the crushed chillies. Bring to the boil and simmer gently for 5–10 minutes until the salsa has thickened slightly. Reserve the salsa to allow the flavours to develop while the pasta is cooking.

Bring a large pan of water to the boil and add the pasta. Simmer gently for 3–4 minutes or until the pasta is just tender. Drain the pasta and rinse in boiling water. Top with a large spoonful of salsa and a small spoonful of yogurt. Garnish, if liked, with the chopped basil and oregano and serve immediately.

This dish is better if eaten immediately. The salsa would keep well in the refrigerator spooned into a small bowl, covered with clingfilm and used in 2–3 days.

TASTY TIP

Add some vegetables, such as chopped courgettes, tiny broccoli florets, thawed peas and sweetcorn. Cook the veg lightly for 3–4 minutes, drain and stir into the cooked pasta before adding the salsa.

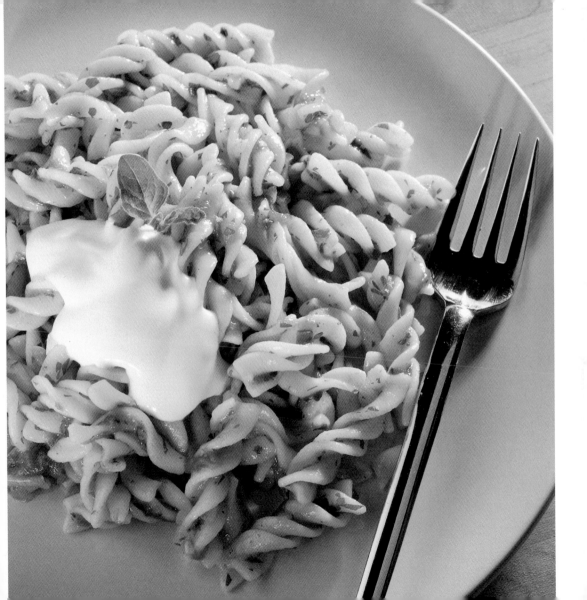

Chicken & Mushroom Lasagne

MAKES 4 PORTIONS

1 tbsp olive or sunflower oil
225 g/8 oz button mushrooms,
  wiped and sliced
15 g/½ oz butter or margarine
25 g/1 oz plain flour
300 ml/½ pint skimmed milk
1 bay leaf
225 g/8 oz cooked
  chicken, cubed

¼ tsp freshly grated
  nutmeg (optional)
salt and freshly ground
  black pepper
400 g can tomatoes,
  drained and chopped
1 tsp dried mixed herbs
9 lasagne sheets
  (about 150 g/5 oz)

For the topping:
200 ml/7 fl oz 0%-fat
  Greek yogurt
1 medium egg,
  lightly beaten
1 tbsp finely grated
  Parmesan cheese
mixed salad leaves,
  to serve

Preheat the oven to 180°C/350°F/Gas 4. Heat the oil and cook the mushrooms until tender and all the juices have evaporated. Remove and reserve. Put the butter or margarine, flour, milk and bay leaf in the pan. Slowly bring to the boil, stirring until thickened. Simmer for 2–3 minutes. Remove the bay leaf and stir in the mushrooms, chicken, nutmeg, salt and pepper.

Mix together the tomatoes, mixed herbs and season with salt and pepper. Spoon half into the base of a 1.7 litre/3 pint ovenproof dish or use four individual dishes. Top with 3 sheets of lasagne, breaking them where necessary to fit. Cover with half the chicken mixture. Repeat the layers, then arrange the remaining 3 sheets of pasta on top. Mix together the yogurt and egg. Spoon over the lasagne, spreading the mixture into the corners. Sprinkle with the Parmesan and bake in the preheated oven for 45 minutes. Serve with the mixed salad.

Any uneaten lasagne can be covered in clingfilm and stored overnight in the refrigerator. If freezing, do so preferably before it is baked: wrap in kitchen foil, label and date. Thaw overnight in the refrigerator and cook as per the recipe. Or, if you prefer to freeze after baking, spoon into small containers and cover, label and date. Keep for up to 1 month. Thaw in the refrigerator overnight. Reheat cooked lasagne in the microwave on a plate covered with clingfilm and pierced 2–3 times, on High for 2 minutes or until piping hot. Allow to stand for 1 minute before eating.

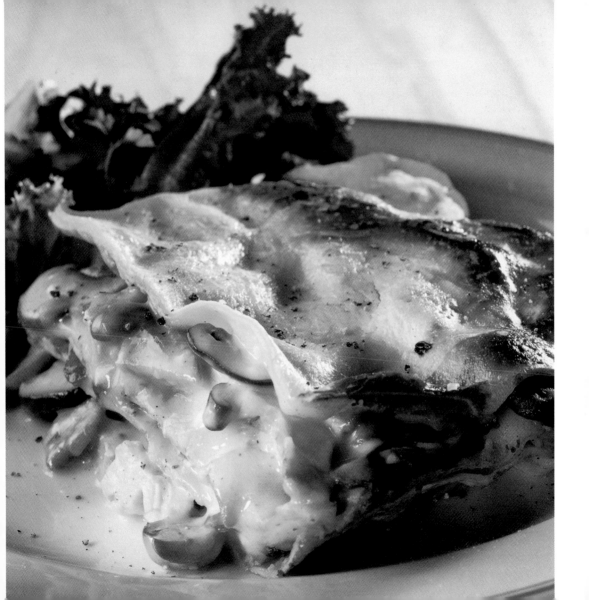

Spaghetti with Turkey & Bacon Sauce

MAKES 1 LARGE PORTION

125 g/4 oz spaghetti
1 tbsp butter or margarine
50 g/2 oz smoked streaky
    bacon, rind removed
75 g/3 oz fresh turkey strips,
    if preferred use chicken

1 small onion, peeled
    and chopped
1 garlic clove, peeled
    and chopped
1 medium egg, beaten
4 tbsp milk

salt and freshly ground
    black pepper
1 tbsp freshly grated
    Parmesan or
    Cheddar cheese
2 tsp freshly chopped
    coriander, to garnish

Bring a large pan of lightly salted water to a rolling boil. Add the spaghetti and cook according to the packet instructions, or until *al dente.*

Meanwhile, melt the butter or margarine in a frying pan. Using a sharp knife cut the streaky bacon into small dice. Add the bacon to the pan with the turkey strips and cook for 8 minutes, or until browned, stirring occasionally to prevent sticking. Add the onion and garlic and cook for 5 minutes, or until softened, stirring occasionally.

Place the egg and milk in a bowl and season to taste with salt and pepper. Beat together then pour into the frying pan and cook, stirring, for 2 minutes or until the mixture begins to thicken but does not scramble.

HELPFUL HINT

It is a good idea to remove the pan from the heat before adding the beaten eggs, as there should be enough residual heat in the sauce to cook them without scrambling them.

Drain the spaghetti thoroughly and return to the pan. Pour over the sauce, add the grated cheese and toss lightly. Heat through for 2 minutes, or until piping hot. Tip into a warmed serving dish and sprinkle with freshly chopped coriander. Serve immediately.

If liked, the sauce can be made ahead so that when a quick meal is required all that has to be done is to cook the pasta and reheat the sauce. Use the sauce within 2 days; it is not suitable for freezing.

Spaghetti & Meatballs

MAKES 1 LARGE PORTION

200 g can tomatoes, chopped
1 tsp tomato purée
1 tsp or to taste, chilli sauce
¼ tsp brown sugar
salt and freshly ground
    black pepper
125 g/4 oz spaghetti

25g/1 oz Cheddar cheese,
    grated, plus extra to serve
freshly chopped parsley,
    to garnish

For the meatballs:
125 g/4 oz lean beef or
    lamb mince

25 g/1 oz fresh breadcrumbs
1 small onion, peeled
    and finely chopped
1 small egg yolk
1 tsp tomato paste
1 tsp freshly chopped parsley
1 tsp freshly
    chopped oregano

HELPFUL HINT

If you do not have a blender or food processor to make the breadcrumbs, make sure that the bread is stale. Discard the crusts and either rub the bread up and down a grater or rub between clean hands.

TASTY TIP

For crisper meatballs, you can fry them instead of baking. Heat 2 tablespoons olive or sunflower oil in a large frying pan and cook over a medium heat for about 15 minutes, turning occasionally, until well-browned.

Preheat the oven to 200°C/400°F/Gas Mark 6, 15 minutes before using. Place the chopped tomatoes, tomato purée, chilli sauce and sugar in a saucepan. Season to taste with salt and pepper and bring to the boil. Cover and simmer for 15 minutes, then cook, uncovered, for a further 5 minutes, or until the sauce has reduced and thickened.

Meanwhile, make the meatballs. Place the ingredients in a bowl and mix together until well blended. Shape the mixture into small balls, about the size of an apricot, and place on an oiled baking tray. Cook in the preheated oven for 20 minutes, or until browned and cooked.

Meanwhile, bring a large pan of lightly salted water to a rolling boil. Add the pasta and cook according to the packet instructions, or until *al dente*. Drain the pasta and return to the pan. Pour over the tomato sauce and toss gently to coat. Tip into a warmed serving dish and top with the meatballs. Garnish with chopped parsley and serve immediately with grated cheese.

The sauce and meatballs can be kept in the refrigerator for up to 2 days. Place separately in small bowls and cover with clingfilm. Or, freeze, in separate containers, labelled and dated, for up to 1 month. Thaw in the refrigerator. Reheat separately. The meatballs can be either gently fried in a little oil or cooked in the microwave for 2 minutes. The sauce will reheat in a small saucepan or the microwave. Cook fresh pasta. Make sure it is all piping hot before eating.

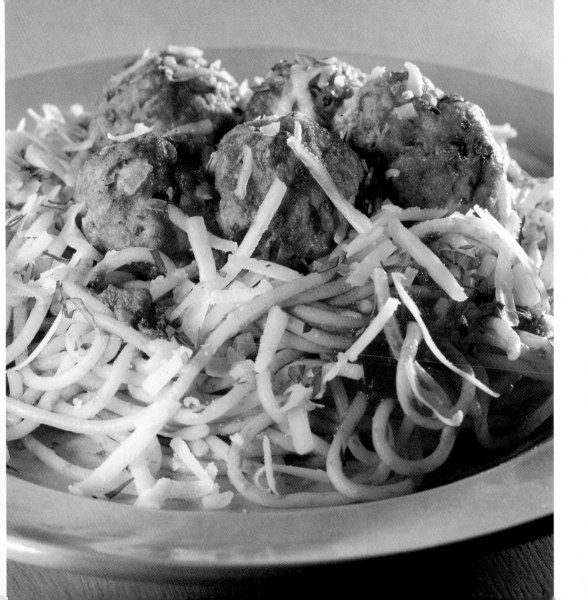

Spaghetti Bolognese

MAKES 1 LARGE PORTION

1 tbsp olive or sunflower oil
2 rashers unsmoked streaky
   bacon, rind removed
   and chopped
1 small onion, peeled
   and finely chopped
1 small carrot, peeled
   and finely chopped

½ celery stalk, trimmed and
   finely chopped
1 garlic clove, peeled
   and crushed
1 bay leaf (optional)
125 g/4 oz beef mince
200 g can tomatoes,
   chopped

1–2 tsp tomato purée
150 ml/¼ pint beef stock
salt and freshly ground
   black pepper
125 g/ 4 oz spaghetti
freshly grated Parmesan
   or Cheddar cheese,
   to serve

Heat the olive or sunflower oil in a heavy-based pan, add the bacon and cook for 5 minutes or until slightly coloured. Add the onion, carrot, celery, garlic and bay leaf, if using, and cook, stirring, for 8 minutes, or until the vegetables are soft.

Add the beef mince to the pan and cook, stirring with a wooden spoon to break up any lumps in the meat, for 5–8 minutes, or until browned.

Stir the tomatoes and tomato purée into the mince and pour in the stock. Bring to the boil, lower the heat and simmer for 20 minutes, stirring occasionally. The longer you leave the sauce to cook, the more intense the flavour. Season to taste with salt and pepper and remove the bay leaf, if used.

Meanwhile, bring a large pan of lightly salted water to a rolling boil, add the spaghetti and cook for about 8 minutes or until *al dente*. Drain and arrange on warmed serving plates. Top with the prepared Bolognese sauce and serve immediately sprinkled with grated cheese.

The Bolognese sauce will keep well in the refrigerator covered with clingfilm for up to 3 days or will freeze, in a lidded containr, for 1 month. Reheat in a saucepan until piping hot, or cover with clingfilm, pierce 2–3 times and heat on High in the microwave for 2 minutes or until piping hot.

FOOD FACT

Bolognese sauce, or *ragù alla Bolognese*, is enjoyed throughout the world. It originated in the city of Bologna in Emilia-Romagna, where it is always served with tagliatelle, not spaghetti.

Lasagne

MAKES 4 PORTIONS

4 quantities prepared
    Bolognese sauce
    (*see* page 156)
75 g/3 oz butter or
    margarine
4 tbsp plain flour

750 ml/1¼ pints milk
1 tsp readymade mustard
salt and freshly ground
    black pepper
9 sheets lasagne

50g/2oz freshly grated
    Parmesan or
    Cheddar cheese
freshly chopped parsley, to
    garnish (optional)
garlic bread, to serve

Preheat the oven to 200˚C/400˚F/Gas Mark 6, 15 minutes before cooking. Stir the prepared Bolognese sauce and reserve.

Melt the butter or margarine in a small heavy-based pan, add the flour and cook gently, stirring, for 2 minutes. Remove from the heat and gradually stir in the milk. Return to the heat and cook, stirring, for 2 minutes, or until the sauce thickens. Bring to the boil, remove from the heat and stir in the mustard. Season to taste with salt and pepper. Butter a rectangular ovenproof dish and spread a thin layer of the white sauce over the base. Cover completely with 3 sheets of lasagne. Spoon a third of the prepared Bolognese sauce over the lasagne. Spoon over a third of the remaining white sauce, then sprinkle with a third of the grated cheese. Repeat the layers, finishing with cheese. Bake in the preheated oven for 30 minutes, or until golden-brown. Garnish, if liked, and serve immediately with warm garlic bread.

Store any uneaten lasagne in the refrigerator for up to 2 days. Spoon onto a clean plate or dish trying not to disturb the layers. Cover with clingfilm. Reheat in the microwave, covered with fresh clingfilm and heat on high for 2 minutes. Allow to stand for at least 1 minute before eating. If you want to freeze, this recipe will freeze well, but I would recommend freezing whole, unbaked (perfect for when parents are coming to visit). Make the recipe as above, but don't bake, then freeze for up to 1 month. It would be better to open freeze then wrap, label and date. When ready to eat, thaw overnight in the refrigerator and bake as above.

Sausage & Redcurrant Pasta Bake

MAKES 1 PORTION

2 good quality, thick
    pork sausages
1 tsp sunflower or olive oil
1 small onion, peeled
    and sliced
2 tsp plain white flour

300 ml/½ pint chicken stock
1 tsp freshly chopped thyme
    leaves, plus sprigs
    to garnish
1 bay leaf (optional)
4 tsp redcurrant jelly

salt and freshly ground
    black pepper
125 g/4 oz fresh penne
1 tbsp grated cheese

HELPFUL HINT

When buying sausages, buy a
few and freeze in portions.
When wishing to use, thaw
overnight in the refrigerator
and use as required. Do not
re-freeze unless they have
been cooked first.

Prick the sausages, place under a preheated grill and cook for 15 minutes, turning frequently. Alternatively, cook them on the hob in a nonstick frying pan for 15 minutes, turning frequently or until golden brown. (There is no need when cooking sausages to use any oil or fat. During cooking the fat in the sausages will be enough.) Reserve and wipe the frying pan clean if necessary.

Heat the oil in the frying pan, add the sliced onion and fry for 5 minutes, or until golden-brown. Stir in the flour and cook for 2 minutes. Remove the pan from the heat and gradually stir in the chicken stock. Return the pan to the heat and bring to the boil, stirring continuously until the sauce starts to thicken. Add the thyme, bay leaf, if using, and redcurrant jelly and season well with salt and pepper. Simmer the sauce for 3 minutes.

Bring a large pan of salted water to a rolling boil, add the pasta and cook for about 4 minutes, or until *al dente*. Drain thoroughly and reserve. Heat the oven to 200°C/400°F/Gas Mark 6 and place the sausages in an ovenproof dish. Add the pasta then pour over the sauce, removing the bay leaf, if used, and toss together. Sprinkle with the cheese and cook in the oven for 15–20 minutes, or until bubbling and golden-brown. Serve immediately, garnished with thyme sprigs.

The sauce and sausages will keep well overnight in the refrigerator, covered. To finish the dish, prepare with the pasta and cheese as above, cover with kitchen foil and cook in the oven for 25 minutes, removing the foil for the last 10 minutes so that the cheese browns and bubbles.

Essential Curries

Chicken & Lentil Curry

MAKES 1 LARGE PORTION

2–3 chicken thighs, depending
    on appetite, skinned
2 tsp sunflower or
    vegetable oil
40 g/1½ oz split red lentils
2–3 tsp mild curry paste
1 bay leaf (optional)

small strip of lemon zest
300 ml/½ pint chicken or
    vegetable stock
40 g/1½ oz spinach leaves,
    rinsed; shredded, if liked
1 tsp freshly chopped
    coriander (optional)

2 tsp lemon juice
salt and freshly ground
    black pepper

To serve:
freshly cooked rice
low-fat natural yogurt

Secure the chicken thighs with cocktail sticks to keep their shape. Heat the oil in a nonstick frying pan, add the chicken and fry for 5 minutes, turning frequently until browned all over, remove from the pan and reserve.

Put the lentils in a sieve and rinse thoroughly under cold running water. Place in a saucepan then stir in the curry paste, bay leaf, if using, lemon zest and stock. Stir, and then slowly bring to the boil. Turn down the heat to a gentle simmer, half-cover the pan with a lid and cook for 5 minutes, stirring occasionally. Place the chicken in the pan with the lentils and half-cover. Simmer for 20 minutes. Stir in the spinach and cook for a further 5 minutes or until the chicken is very tender and the sauce is thick. Remove the bay leaf, if using, and lemon zest. Stir in the coriander and lemon juice, then season to taste with salt and pepper. Serve immediately with the rice and a little natural yogurt.

Any leftover curry can be kept, covered with clingfilm, in the refrigerator overnight. Ensure that the chicken is thoroughly reheated before eating. Reheat if possible in the microwave. Cover with fresh clingfilm, pierce the film 2–3 times and heat on High for 3 minutes 20 seconds. Allow to stand for 2 minutes before eating. If not using a microwave, place the curry in a saucepan and bring to the boil. Reduce to a simmer, cover with a lid and cook for 10–12 minutes, stirring frequently to prevent it burning before eating; ensure that it is piping hot.

HELPFUL HINT

It's useful to know chicken cuts: breast and fillet are good for stir-frying, pan frying and grilling; thighs and drumsticks are for stews and casseroles; portions are for roasting and casseroles.

Spinach Dhal

MAKES 1 LARGE PORTION

40 g/1½ oz split red lentils
1 small onion, peeled
   and chopped
50 g/2 oz potato, peeled and
   cut into small chunks

½ green chilli, deseeded
   and chopped
150 ml/¼ pint water
½ tsp turmeric
125 g/4 oz fresh spinach

1 medium tomato,
   chopped
2 tsp vegetable oil
1 tsp mustard seeds
   (optional)

Rinse the lentils and place in a saucepan with the onion, potato, chilli, water and turmeric. Bring to the boil, then reduce the heat, cover and simmer for 15 minutes, or until the lentils are tender and most of the liquid has been absorbed.

Chop the spinach and add to the pan with the tomato and cook for a further 5 minutes, or until the spinach has wilted.

Heat the oil in a frying pan, add the mustard seeds, and fry for 1 minute, or until they pop. Stir into the dhal and serve.

The dhal will keep well if placed in a clean bowl, covered with clingfilm and left in the refrigerator. Use within 3 days.

To freeze, place the cooked dhal in a container or freezer bag and place in the freezer, not forgetting to label and date. Keep for up to 1 month. When ready to eat, thaw completely overnight in the refrigerator then heat on High for 2 minutes, stirring halfway through the reheating time. Alternatively, reheat in a saucepan over a low heat, stirring frequently, for 5–8 minutes. Ensure the dhal is piping hot before eating.

HELPFUL HINT

It is important that spices are stored correctly otherwise their flavour can be impaired. Unless you use a lot, buy in small quantities and store in a cool dark place. If you have time, grind your own to give more flavour and aroma.

Lamb & Potato Curry

MAKES 2 PORTIONS

175 g/ 6 oz boneless lamb, such as neck of lamb fillet
1 tbsp vegetable oil
1 onion, peeled and cut into wedges
1–2 garlic cloves, peeled and sliced
1 celery stalk, trimmed and sliced (optional)

2–3 tsp Madras curry powder, or to taste
1 tsp tomato purée
150 ml/¼ pint water
150 ml/¼ pint coconut milk (optional)
2 tomatoes, chopped
175 g/6 oz new potatoes, scrubbed

50 g/2 oz carrots, peeled and sliced

To serve:
freshly cooked rice
naan bread
natural yogurt

Discard any fat or gristle from the lamb, then cut into thin strips and reserve. Heat the oil in a deep frying pan; add the onion, garlic and celery, if using, and fry for 5 minutes, or until softened. Add the curry powder and continue to fry for a further 2 minutes, stirring constantly. Add the lamb and cook for 5 minutes, or until coated in the curry paste.

Blend the tomato purée with the water then stir into the pan together with the coconut milk, if using, and chopped tomatoes. (If not using coconut milk use either more water or stock.) Cut the potatoes into small chunks and add to the pan with the carrots. Bring to the boil, then reduce the heat, cover and simmer for 30–35 minutes until the lamb and vegetables are tender. Serve with freshly cooked rice, naan bread and natural yogurt to give a creamy taste.

The curry will keep well, so keep the other portion in the refrigerator, spooned into a clean bowl and covered with clingfilm. Eat within 2 days. Or, place in a container or freezer bag, label and date and freeze. Use within 1 month. To reheat, place the chilled or thawed curry in a saucepan, bring to the boil, cover with a lid and reduce the heat to a simmer. Cook, stirring frequently, for 10–12 minutes or until piping hot. Or, place the curry into a clean bowl, cover with clingfilm, pierce 2–3 times then heat on High in the microwave for 3 minutes. Stir, then allow to stand for 1 minute. Ensure the curry is piping hot.

Thai Green Chicken Curry

MAKES 2 PORTIONS

1 small onion, peeled and chopped
1 lemon grass stalk, outer leaves discarded and finely sliced (optional)
1 garlic clove, peeled and finely chopped
1 tbsp freshly grated root ginger

1 green chilli
zest and juice of ½ lemon
2 tbsp groundnut or vegetable oil
1–2 tsp Thai fish sauce (optional)
1 tbsp freshly chopped coriander
1 tbsp freshly chopped basil

175 g/6 oz skinless, boneless chicken breasts cut into strips
50 g /2 oz fine green beans, trimmed
200 ml can coconut milk
fresh basil leaves, to garnish (optional)
freshly cooked rice, to serve

Place the onion, lemon grass, if using, garlic, ginger, chilli, lemon zest and juice, 1 tablespoon of the oil, the fish sauce, if using, coriander and basil in a bowl. Using a handheld blender (or food processor), blend to a form a smooth paste, which should be of a spoonable consistency. If the sauce looks thick, add a little water. Remove and reserve.

Heat the wok or large frying pan, add the remaining 1 tablespoon of oil and, when hot, add the chicken. Stir-fry for 2–3 minutes, until the chicken starts to colour, then add the green beans and stir-fry for a further minute. Remove the chicken and beans from the wok or frying pan and reserve. Wipe the wok or frying pan clean with absorbent kitchen paper.

TASTY TIP

One tablespoon extra lemon zest can be used in place of the lemon grass stalk.

Spoon the reserved green paste into the wok or frying pan and heat for 1 minute. Add the coconut milk and whisk to blend. Return the chicken and beans to the wok or frying pan and bring to the boil. Simmer for 5–7 minutes, or until the chicken is cooked. Sprinkle with basil leaves, if using, and serve immediately with freshly cooked rice.

This curry would be super to share with a friend, but it can be kept overnight in the refrigerator in a clean bowl. Cover with clingfilm and use within 2 days. I would not recommend freezing, as the delicate flavour could be lost.

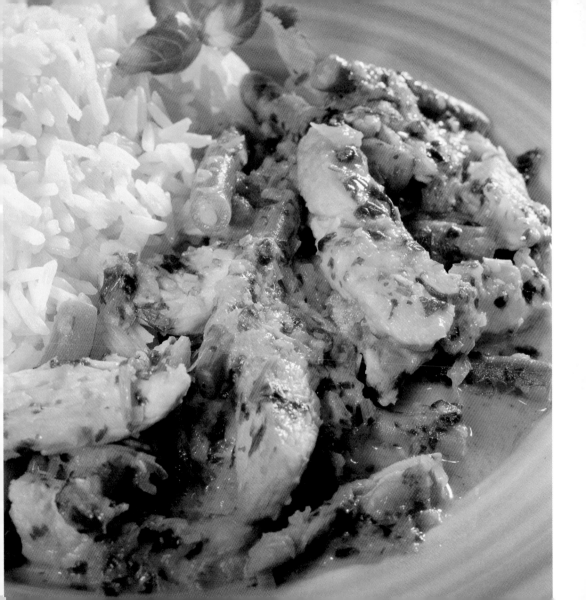

Kerala Pork Curry

MAKES 1 LARGE PORTION

125 g/4 oz lean pork such as
   fillet or loin, trimmed
1 tbsp vegetable oil
2 tsp desiccated coconut
1 tsp mustard seeds
1 cinnamon stick, bruised
½ tsp ground cumin
½ tsp ground coriander

1 red chilli, deseeded
   and chopped
1–2 garlic cloves, peeled
   and chopped
1 small onion, peeled
   and chopped
½ tsp saffron strands
   or turmeric

150 ml/¼ pint coconut milk,
   or use a small piece of
   creamed coconut blended
   with warm water
50 ml/2 fl oz water
50 g/2 oz frozen peas
freshly cooked basmati
   rice, to serve

Cut the pork into small chunks and reserve. Heat 1 teaspoon of the oil in a frying pan; add the desiccated coconut and fry for 30 seconds, stirring, until lightly toasted. Reserve.

Add the remaining oil to the pan, add the seeds and fry for 30 seconds, or until they pop. Add the remaining spices and cook, stirring, for 2 minutes. Add the pork and fry for 5 minutes, or until sealed. Add the chilli, garlic and onion and continue to fry for 3 minutes before stirring in the saffron or turmeric blended with a teaspoon of water. Stir, then pour in the coconut milk and water. Bring to the boil then reduce the heat, cover and simmer, stirring occasionally, for 30 minutes. Add a little more water if the liquid is evaporating quickly. Turn the heat down slightly, then add the peas and cook for a further 10 minutes before serving with freshly cooked basmati rice.

If you have some of this delicious curry left, spoon into a bowl, cover with clingfilm and keep for up to two days in the refrigerator. To reheat, re-cover the bowl with clean clingfilm and heat on High for 2 minutes 20 seconds in the microwave until piping hot, allowing to stand for 2 minutes before stirring and serving. Or, reheat in a saucepan: spoon into the pan, place over a gentle heat and bring to the boil; reduce the heat to a simmer, cover with a lid and cook for 10–12 minutes, stirring frequently, until piping hot. Add a little extra water if drying out. The curry will freeze, but the flavour will not be so intense. Keep in the freezer no longer than 1 month.

Tarka Dhal

MAKES 1 LARGE PORTION

1–2 green chillies
50 g/2 oz red split lentils
75 g/3 oz yellow split lentils
1 small onion, peeled
and chopped

1–2 garlic cloves, peeled
and sliced
1 medium tomato, chopped
½ tsp turmeric
450 ml/¾ pint water

2 tsp vegetable oil
½ tsp cumin seeds or
ground cumin
2 tsp freshly chopped
coriander

Deseed the chillies and chop. Rinse the lentils then place in a large saucepan with the onion, half of the sliced garlic cloves, the chillies, tomato, turmeric and water. Bring to the boil, then reduce the heat, cover and simmer for 20 minutes. Remove the lid and cook for a further 5 minutes.

Heat the oil in a frying pan; add the seeds, if using, and remaining sliced garlic. Sprinkle in the ground cumin, if using, and cook for 1–2 minutes, or until lightly browned.

Place the cooked lentil mixture into a warmed serving bowl, stir in the chopped coriander and sprinkle the toasted seeds and garlic on top. Serve.

Any remaining dhal will keep very well in the refrigerator for up to 3 days. Place in a clean bowl, cover with clingfilm. It would freeze too, if you prefer. Spoon the dhal into a freezer bag, label and date. Keep for up to 1 month and thaw in the refrigerator.

When ready to reheat, place in a clean bowl, cover with clingfilm, pierce 2–3 times and cook on High in the microwave for 2 minutes. Allow to stand for 1 minute, stir well, then eat. Or, place into a clean saucepan and place over a gentle heat. Cook, stirring, for 5–8 minutes, adding a little water if too thick; stir before eating.

FOOD FACT

Dhal is a thick soup-like dish and nearly always contains lentils and usually another pulse as well. It can be eaten by itself or as a side dish.

Curried Potatoes with Spinach

MAKES 1 LARGE PORTION

150 g/5 oz potatoes, peeled
½ tsp cumin seeds or
ground cumin
2 tsp vegetable oil
1 small onion, peeled
and chopped

1 garlic clove, peeled
and crushed
½–1 red chilli, depending on
heat tolerance, deseeded
and finely chopped
½ tsp ground coriander
½ tsp turmeric

2 medium tomatoes
125 g/ 4 oz fresh leaf
spinach, lightly rinsed
and chopped
25 ml/1 fl oz water
1–2 tsp salt and freshly
ground black pepper

Cut the potatoes into small cubes and reserve. Dry-fry the cumin seeds, if using, in a saucepan for 30 seconds, then add the oil, potatoes and ground cumin, if using. Cook for 3–5 minutes, stirring, or until the potatoes are beginning to turn golden.

Add the onion, garlic and chilli and continue to cook for 2–3 minutes, or until the onion is beginning to soften. Sprinkle in the ground coriander and turmeric and cook for a further 2 minutes.

Chop the tomatoes and stir into the pan. Cover and cook, stirring occasionally, for 10 minutes, or until the potatoes are tender. Stir in the spinach, water and seasoning, to taste, and cook for 2 minutes, or until the spinach has wilted, then serve.

Any leftover potatoes can be kept overnight in the refrigerator. Place in a clean dish and cover with clingfilm. They would not freeze well. They can then be reheated in the microwave covered with clean clingfilm, which has been pierced 2–3 times – heat on High for 1 minute or until piping hot. Or, they could be fried in a little oil, stirring frequently, for 5 minutes. They would also be good if eaten cold.

TASTY TIP

This is an ideal accompaniment for all curries as well as being a good snack for lunch or supper.

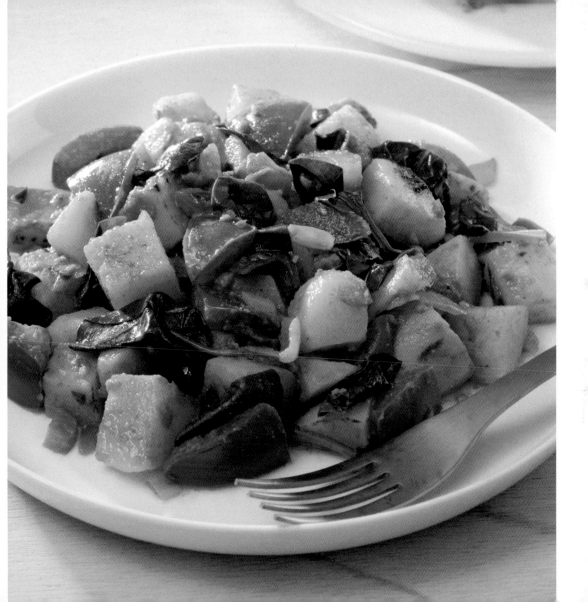

Malaysian Fish Curry

MAKES 2 PORTIONS

2 firm fish fillets, such as
    fresh haddock or coley,
    125 g/4 oz each in weight
1 tbsp groundnut or
    vegetable oil
2 garlic cloves, peeled
    and crushed
2.5 cm/1 inch piece fresh root
    ginger, peeled and grated

1 tsp turmeric
1 tsp ground coriander
1 tbsp mild or medium
    Madras curry paste,
    depending on taste
250 ml/8 fl oz coconut milk
1 tbsp freshly chopped
    coriander

lime or lemon wedges, to
    garnish (optional)
stir-fried oriental vegetables
    and fragrant rice, to serve

Preheat the oven to 180°C/350°F/Gas Mark 4. Lightly rinse the fish fillets and pat dry with absorbent kitchen paper. Place in a lightly oiled ovenproof dish.

Heat the oil in a frying pan, add the garlic and ginger and fry for 2 minutes. Add the turmeric, ground coriander and curry paste and cook for a further 3 minutes, stirring frequently. Take off the heat and gradually stir in the coconut milk. Cool slightly, then pour over the fish. Cover with lightly buttered kitchen foil and cook in the preheated oven for 20 minutes, or until the fish is tender. Sprinkle with chopped coriander, and then garnish with lime or lemon wedges, if using, and serve with stir-fried vegetables and freshly cooked rice.

If liked, one of the cooked fillets could be kept to eat the next day. Cook and allow to cool before covering with clingfilm and placing in the refrigerator overnight. Or, the cooked fish could be frozen, but the flavour will not be as intense. If wishing to freeze, wrap in kitchen foil, label, date and freeze for up to 1 month. To reheat, ensure the fish is thoroughly thawed if frozen. Place on a plate, cover with clingfilm and pierce 2–3 times. Heat on High for 1 minute 20 seconds, allow to stand for 1 minute, then eat.

HELPFUL HINT
Do use a mild- or medium-heat curry paste – a really hot curry paste will destroy the delicate taste of the fish.

Lamb Balti

MAKES 2 PORTIONS

225 g/8 oz lean lamb, such
    as neck fillet, trimmed
2 tsp vegetable oil
1 tsp mustard seeds (optional)
½ tsp ground coriander
½ tsp ground cumin
½ tsp turmeric
½ tsp garam masala

1–2 garlic cloves, peeled
    and crushed
1–2 green chillies, depending
    on heat tolerance,
    deseeded and chopped
1 onion, peeled and chopped
½–1 small aubergine,
    trimmed and chopped

2 tomatoes, chopped
1 tsp tomato purée
450 ml/¾ pint lamb or
    vegetable stock
2 tsp freshly
    chopped coriander
naan bread, to serve

Dice the lamb and reserve. Heat the oil in a large frying pan, add the mustard seeds, if using, and fry for 30 seconds, or until they pop.

Add the remaining spices to the pan and cook for 2 minutes, stirring throughout, before adding the garlic, chillies, onion and aubergine. Cook, stirring, for a further 5 minutes, or until the vegetables are coated in the spices.

Add the lamb and continue to fry for 5–8 minutes, or until sealed. Stir in the chopped tomatoes. Blend the tomato purée with the stock then pour into the pan. Bring to the boil, cover, reduce the heat and simmer for 45–50 minutes, or until the lamb is tender. Sprinkle with chopped coriander and serve with plenty of naan bread.

TASTY TIP

It is often a good idea to
make extra curry, as the
flavour will intensify if
left overnight.

Any remaining balti will keep well overnight in the refrigerator. Spoon into a clean bowl, cover with clingfilm and place in the refrigerator. It will also freeze well. Keep for up to 1 month. Reheat in the microwave on High for 2 minutes 30 seconds. Stand for 1 minute; if not piping hot, reheat for a further minute, stand for 1 minute then eat. Or, reheat in a saucepan on the hob for 10–12 minutes, stir well and ensure it is piping hot before eating. Balti is meant to be a wet curry so if there is not much liquid when reheating add a little water or stock.

Caribbean–style Chicken Stew

MAKES 2 PORTIONS

4 skinless, boneless chicken portions, each about 125 g/4 oz in weight
1 tbsp groundnut or vegetable oil
1 celery stalk, trimmed (optional)
3 baby onions, peeled and halved

1–2 garlic cloves, peeled and sliced
½ habanero chilli, deseeded and sliced or ½–1 tsp dried crushed chillies
½ tsp ground cumin
¼ tsp ground coriander
½ tsp turmeric
2 tsp demerara sugar

2 medium tomatoes, chopped
450 ml/¾ pint chicken stock
1 tsp freshly chopped coriander
sweet potato mash (optional) to serve

Lightly rinse the chicken and dry with absorbent kitchen paper. Heat the oil in a large saucepan or frying pan add the chicken and brown on all sides. Remove and reserve.

Chop the celery and add to the pan with the onions, garlic and chilli. Fry for 5–8 minutes then add all the spices and cook for a further 3 minutes. Add the sugar, tomatoes and stock and bring to the boil.

Return the chicken to the pan, then reduce the heat, cover and simmer for 1 hour, or until the chicken is tender. Spoon into a warmed serving dish, sprinkle with chopped coriander and serve with the sweet potato mash, if using.

Any remaining chicken can be kept in the refrigerator overnight. Place on a clean plate and cover with clingfilm. Use within 2 days. It will also freeze for up to 1 month. Place in a freezer bag, label and date. Thaw in the refrigerator.

To reheat, place the chicken in a saucepan with a lid. Heat on the hob for 10–12 minutes until piping hot.

HELPFUL HINT

When reheating chicken it is very important to ensure that it is thoroughly reheated until piping hot.

Chicken & Chickpea Korma

MAKES 2 PORTIONS

175 g/6 oz skinless,
  boneless chicken
1 tbsp vegetable oil
1 medium onion, peeled
  and cut into wedges
1–2 garlic cloves, peeled
  and chopped

1–2 tbsp Korma curry paste
½–1 tsp ground cloves
450 ml/¾ pint chicken stock
2 medium ripe tomatoes,
  peeled and chopped
210 g can chickpeas,
  drained and rinsed

2 tbsp double cream,
  or use coconut milk
3 spring onions, trimmed
  and diagonally sliced
Indian-style bread,
  to serve

Cut the chicken into small strips and reserve. Heat the oil in a wok or frying pan; add the chicken and cook, stirring, for 3 minutes, or until sealed. Remove and reserve.

Add the onion and garlic to the pan and fry gently for 5 minutes, or until the onion has begun to soften. Add the curry paste and ground cloves and cook, stirring, for 2 minutes. Return the chicken to the pan and stir well.

Add the stock, tomatoes and chickpeas, then bring to the boil, reduce and simmer for 15–20 minutes, or until the chicken is cooked. Stir in the cream or coconut milk. Spoon into a warmed serving dish, sprinkle with the spring onions and serve with Indian-style bread.

Any remaining curry can be kept in the refrigerator for up to 2 days or frozen for up to 1 month. Place the curry in a bowl, covered with clingfilm, and keep in the refrigerator or place in a freezer bag, label, date and freeze.

When reheating chicken it is very important to ensure that the chicken is thoroughly reheated. Place the chicken in a saucepan with a lid. Heat on the hob for 10–12 minutes until piping hot. Or, reheat in the microwave. Heat on High for 2 minutes and allow to stand for 1 minute. Check that the curry is piping hot, if not, heat for a further 1 minute.

Creamy Vegetable Korma

MAKES 1 LARGE PORTION

1 tbsp butter or vegetable oil
1 small onion, peeled
   and chopped
1 garlic clove, peeled
   and crushed
small piece root ginger,
   peeled and grated
1 tsp ground coriander
½ tsp ground cumin

½ tsp ground turmeric
finely grated zest and juice
   of ½ lemon
15 g/½ oz ground almonds
300 ml/½ pint vegetable stock
125 g/4 oz potatoes,
   peeled and diced
75 g/3 oz mixed vegetables,
   such as cauliflower,

carrots and turnip,
   cut into chunks
2 tbsp double cream or
   creamed coconut blended
   with 2 tbsp warm water
1 tsp freshly chopped coriander
salt and freshly ground
   black pepper
naan bread, to serve

Heat the butter or oil in a large saucepan. Add the onion and cook for 5 minutes. Stir in the garlic and ginger and cook for a further 5 minutes, or until soft and just beginning to colour.

Stir in the ground coriander, cumin and turmeric. Continue cooking over a low heat for 1 minute, stirring.

Stir in the lemon zest and juice and almonds. Blend in the vegetable stock. Slowly bring to the boil, stirring occasionally.

Add the potatoes and vegetables. Bring back to the boil, then reduce the heat to a gentle simmer, cover and simmer for 25–30 minutes, or until the vegetables are just tender. Check after 20 minutes and add a little more stock if needed.

Slowly stir in the cream or creamed coconut and chopped coriander. Season to taste with salt and pepper. Cook very gently until heated through, but do not boil. Serve immediately with naan bread.

This dish will not keep or reheat very well so only cook the amount you can eat.

Paneer & Pea Curry

MAKES 2 PORTIONS

75 g/3 oz paneer
150 ml/¼ pint vegetable oil,
    for deep frying, plus 1
    tbsp oil
1 onion, peeled and chopped
1 garlic cloves, peeled
    and chopped
½–1 red chilli, deseeded
    and chopped or

¼–½ tsp dried crushed chilli
1–2 tsp medium curry
    powder
2 tomatoes, chopped
150 g/5 oz sugar snap peas
    or 75 g/3 oz thawed frozen
    garden peas
50 ml/2 fl oz water (optional)

2 tbsp double cream or
    small piece creamed
    coconut dissolved in
    2 tbsp warm water
2 tsp freshly chopped
    coriander (optional)

Cut the paneer into small cubes. Heat the oil in a deep fryer to a temperature of 180°C/350°F then deep-fry the paneer cubes for 3–4 minutes, or until golden brown. Drain on absorbent kitchen paper and reserve.

Heat 1 tablespoon of oil in a frying pan; add the onion, garlic and chilli and fry for 5 minutes, stirring frequently, until slightly softened. Sprinkle in the curry powder.

Stir in the chopped tomatoes and peas and continue to cook for 10 minutes, or until the peas are tender. Stir in a little water if the mixture is getting too dry. Add the fried paneer and heat for 2–3 minutes before stirring in the cream or coconut. Heat gently for 2–3 minutes, then stir in the chopped coriander, if using. Serve.

This dish will not keep or reheat very well so only cook the amount you can eat, or invite a friend round to share.

FOOD FACT

Paneer cheese is perhaps India's most well-known cheese. It has a firm texture and works well when fried, grilled or pan-fried.

Egg & Aubergine Curry

MAKES 1 LARGE PORTION

2 medium eggs
1 tbsp vegetable oil
1 onion, peeled and chopped
1 garlic clove, finely chopped
½–1 green chilli, deseeded
   and finely chopped
small piece fresh root
   ginger, peeled and grated

1 tsp medium hot
   curry powder
½ tsp turmeric
½ tsp ground coriander
125 g/4 oz baby aubergines
   trimmed or 1 small
   aubergine

200 g/7 oz canned
   tomatoes, chopped
2 tbsp double cream or
   small piece creamed
   coconut blended with
   2 tbsp water
1 tbsp freshly
   chopped coriander

Place the eggs in a saucepan and cover with cold water. Bring to the boil and continue to boil for 10 minutes. Drain and plunge into cold water and leave until cold. Drain, shell and reserve.

Heat the oil in a saucepan, add the onions, garlic, chilli and ginger and cook for 5 minutes, or until the onion has softened. Add the spices and continue to cook for a further 5 minutes.

Halve the baby aubergines, or chop the small aubergine into chunks, and add to the pan with the chopped tomatoes then simmer gently, stirring occasionally, for 12–15 minutes, or until the aubergine is tender. Stir in the cream or coconut milk and cook for a further 3 minutes. Cut the eggs into quarters, add to the pan and stir gently. Heat for 2 minutes before sprinkling with chopped coriander and serving.

This dish will not keep or reheat very well so only cook the amount you can eat.

Sweet Potato Curry

MAKES 1 LARGE PORTION

1 tbsp vegetable oil
½–1 green chilli, deseeded and chopped
small piece fresh root ginger, peeled and grated
1 tsp curry powder
1 small onion, peeled and cut into wedges

1 large garlic clove, peeled and crushed
175 g/6 oz sweet potatoes, peeled and cut into small chunks
½ green pepper, deseeded and chopped
2 medium tomatoes, chopped

150 ml/¼ pint coconut milk, or a small piece of creamed coconut blended with 4 tbsp warm water
75 g/3 oz fresh spinach leaves

Heat the oil in a frying pan or wok; add the chilli, ginger and curry powder and fry for 3 minutes, stirring frequently. Add the onion and garlic and continue to fry for a further 5 minutes, or until the onion has softened.

Add the sweet potatoes and stir until coated in the spices, and then add the green pepper and chopped tomatoes.

Pour in the coconut milk. Bring to the boil, then reduce the heat, cover and simmer for 12–15 minutes, or until the vegetables are cooked. Stir in the spinach and heat for 3 minutes, or until wilted, then serve.

This dish will not keep or reheat very well so only cook the amount you can eat.

HELPFUL HINT

It is not always possible to buy sweet potatoes. If this is so then other root vegetables can be used instead. Try parsnips, swede or ordinary potatoes, or a mixture of all three.

Rice & Noodles

Bean & Cashew Stir Fry

MAKES 1 LARGE PORTION

1 tbsp groundnut or vegetable oil
1 small onion, peeled and finely chopped
1 small celery stalk, trimmed and chopped
small piece fresh root ginger, peeled and grated

1 garlic clove, peeled and crushed
½–1 red chilli, deseeded and finely chopped
75 g/3 oz fine French beans, trimmed and halved
50 g/2 oz mangetout, sliced diagonally into 3

40 g/1½ oz unsalted cashew nuts
1 tsp brown sugar
85 ml/3 fl oz vegetable stock
1 tbsp light soy sauce
1 tbsp lemon juice
freshly chopped coriander, to garnish

Heat a wok or large frying pan, add the oil and, when hot, add the onion and celery and stir-fry gently for 2–3 minutes or until beginning to soften.

Add the ginger, garlic and chilli to the wok or large frying pan and stir-fry for 30 seconds. Stir in the French beans and mangetout together with the cashew nuts and continue to stir-fry for 1–2 minutes, or until the nuts are golden brown.

Dissolve the sugar in the stock, then blend with the lemon juice and soy sauce. Stir into the bean mixture and bring to the boil.

Simmer gently, stirring occasionally for 3–4 minutes, or until the beans and mangetout are tender but still crisp and the sauce has thickened slightly. Transfer to a warmed serving bowl or spoon onto a warmed plate. Sprinkle with freshly chopped coriander and serve immediately.

This stir fry will not reheat well, however, without any rice, one person can easily eat it all.

FOOD FACT

Spicy and warm, fresh coriander features frequently in Chinese and especially Thai dishes. It has a similar appearance to flat leaf parsley, but the flavour is completely different.

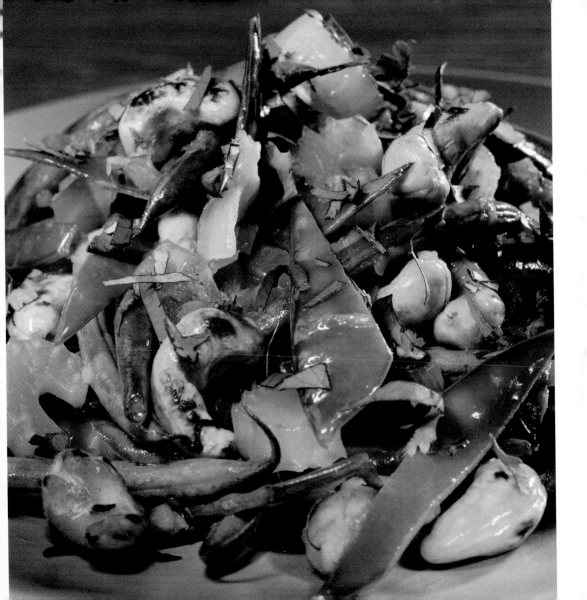

Sweet & Sour Pork

MAKES 1 LARGE PORTION

1 small egg white
2 tsp cornflour
150 g/5oz lean pork, such as
   fillet, trimmed and cubed
300 ml/½ pint vegetable oil
1 small onion, peeled and
   finely cut into sticks
1 medium carrot, peeled
   and cut into matchsticks

small piece fresh root
   ginger, peeled and cut
   into thin strips
85 ml/ 3 fl oz orange juice
85 ml/3 fl oz chicken stock
1 tsp light soy sauce
1 tbsp pineapple pieces
   (from 200 g can), drained
   with juice reserved

1 tsp vinegar or 2 tsp
   lemon juice
1 tsp freshly
   chopped parsley
freshly cooked rice,
   to serve

In a bowl, whisk the egg white and cornflour, then add the pork to the mixture and stir until the cubes are well coated. Heat a wok or large frying pan, then add the oil and heat until very hot before adding the pork and stir-frying for 30 seconds. Turn off the heat and continue to stir for 3 minutes. The meat should be white and sealed. Drain off the oil into a bowl, reserve the pork and wipe the wok or frying pan clean.

Pour 2 teaspoons of the drained oil back into the wok or frying pan and cook the onion, carrot and ginger for 2–3 minutes. Blend the orange juice with the stock, soy sauce and make up to 200 ml/ 7 fl oz with the reserved pineapple juice. Return the pork to the pan with the pineapple juice mixture and simmer for 3–4 minutes. Stir in the pineapple pieces and vinegar or lemon juice. Heat through, then sprinkle with the chopped parsley and serve immediately with freshly cooked rice.

Any remaining pork and sauce can be spooned into a small bowl, covered with clingfilm and kept in the refrigerator; use within 2 days. It could also be frozen with any remaining rice for up to 1 month. If the pork was frozen, ensure that it is thoroughly thawed before reheating. Stir well, then place on a plate with any thawed rice. Cover with clingfilm and pierce the top 2–3 times. Heat on high for 2 minutes. Check the plate feels piping hot underneath. If not, heat for a further minute. Allow to stand for 1 minute, then stir and eat.

TASTY TIP

Any remaining pineapple
can be kept in the refrigerator
in a bowl (not the can) for
up to 3 days.

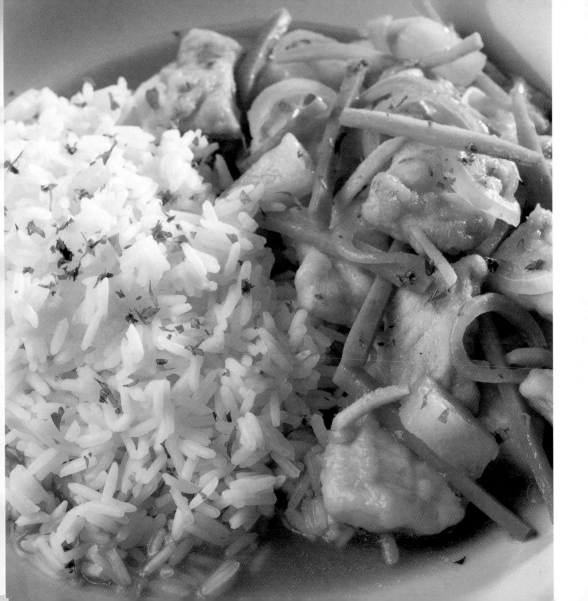

Pad Thai

MAKES 1 LARGE PORTION

50 g/2 oz flat rice noodles
1 tbsp groundnut or
vegetable oil
50 g/2 oz boneless chicken
breast, skinned and
thinly sliced
1 shallot, peeled and
thinly sliced
1 garlic clove, peeled and
finely chopped

2 spring onions, trimmed
and diagonally cut into 5
cm/2 inch pieces
50–75 g/2–3 oz thawed
peeled prawns, chopped,
or fresh white crab meat
25 g/1 oz fresh beansprouts,
rinsed and drained
2 fresh radishes, chopped
1 tbsp roasted peanuts,
chopped (optional)

For the sauce:
½ tbsp Thai fish sauce
(nam pla)
1 tbsp rice vinegar or
malt vinegar
1–2 tsp chilli bean or
oyster sauce
1 tsp toasted sesame oil
1–2 tsp light brown sugar
1 small red chilli, deseeded
and thinly sliced

HELPFUL HINT

Some of the ingredients are
quite expensive in this dish,
so it is perfect for a special
meal. Rice noodles are
usually sold dried, but fresh
are sometimes available.
Check packet instructions.

To make the sauce, whisk all the sauce ingredients in a bowl and reserve. Put the rice noodles in a large bowl and pour over enough hot water to cover. Leave to stand for about 15 minutes until softened. Drain and rinse, then drain again.

Heat the wok or large frying pan until hot but not smoking, then add the oil. Add the chicken strips and stir-fry constantly until they begin to colour. Using a slotted spoon, transfer to a plate. Reduce the heat to medium-high. Add the shallot, garlic and spring onions and stir-fry for 1 minute. Stir in the rice noodles, then the reserved sauce; mix well.

Add the reserved chicken strips with the prawns or crab meat, beansprouts and radish, and stir well. Cook for about 5 minutes, stirring frequently, until heated through. If the noodles begin to stick, add a little water.

Turn into a large shallow serving dish and sprinkle with the chopped peanuts, if using. Serve immediately. I would not recommend keeping.

Rice Nuggets in Herby Tomato Sauce

MAKES 2 PORTIONS

300 ml/½ pint
  vegetable stock
1 bay leaf
75 g/3 oz arborio rice
25 g/1 oz Cheddar
  cheese, grated
1 small egg yolk
1 tsp plain flour

2 tsp freshly chopped parsley
grated Parmesan or extra
  Cheddar cheese, to serve

For the herby tomato sauce:
1 tsp olive oil
1 small onion, peeled and
  thinly sliced

1 garlic clove, peeled
  and crushed
½ small yellow pepper,
  deseeded and diced
200 g can tomatoes,
  chopped
1 tsp freshly chopped basil

HELPFUL HINT

It is important that the stock is absorbed completely by the rice if these nuggets are to hold their shape. Stir all the time for the last minute of cooking to prevent the rice from sticking or burning.

Pour the stock into a large saucepan. Add the bay leaf. Bring to the boil, add the rice, stir, then cover and simmer for 15 minutes. Uncover, reduce the heat to low and cook for a further 5 minutes until the rice is tender and all the stock is absorbed, stirring frequently towards the end of cooking time. Cool. Remove the bay leaf. Stir the cheese, egg yolk, flour and parsley into the rice. Season to taste, then shape into 10 walnut-sized balls. Cover and refrigerate.

To make the sauce, heat the oil in a large frying pan and cook the onion for 5 minutes. Add the garlic and yellow pepper and cook for a further 5 minutes, until soft. Stir in the chopped tomatoes and simmer gently for 3 minutes. Stir in the chopped basil. Add the rice nuggets to the sauce and simmer for a further 10 minutes, or until the nuggets are cooked through and the sauce has reduced a little. Spoon onto plates and serve hot, sprinkled with grated cheese.

Any leftover nuggets can be kept in the refrigerator. Place in a dish with the sauce, cover with clingfilm and use within 2 days. Reheat the nuggets in the microwave on High for 2 minutes, allow to stand for 1 minute and eat while still hot. Or, cover with kitchen foil and reheat in a moderate oven (180°C/350°F/Gas Mark 4) for 20–25 minutes. Stir the sauce occasionally and do not allow it to dry out – add a little stock or water if necessary.

Royal Fried Rice

SERVES 2

75 g/3 oz Thai fragrant rice
1 medium egg
1 tsp sesame or olive oil
salt and freshly ground
    black pepper
2 tbsp groundnut or
    vegetable oil
½ small red pepper, deseeded
    and finely diced

½ small yellow pepper,
    deseeded and finely diced
½ small green pepper,
    deseeded and finely diced
1 small red onion, peeled
    and diced
25 g/1 oz sweetcorn kernels
25 g/1 oz cooked peeled
    prawns, thawed if frozen

25 g/1 oz white crab meat,
    drained if canned, or
    extra prawns
¼ tsp sugar
1–2 tsp light soy sauce

To garnish (optional):
radish rose (*see* page 220)
snipped and whole chive leaves

Rinse the rice in a sieve under cold water, then drain. Place in a saucepan and add twice the volume of water, stirring briefly. Bring to the boil, cover and simmer gently for 15 minutes without further stirring. If the rice has fully absorbed the water while covered, add a little more water. Continue to simmer, uncovered, for another 5 minutes, or until the rice is fully cooked and the water has been absorbed. Leave to cool. Place the egg, sesame or olive oil and a pinch of salt in a small bowl. Using a fork, mix just to break the egg. Reserve. Heat a frying pan or wok and add 1 tablespoon of the groundnut or vegetable oil. When very hot, stir-fry the peppers, onion and sweetcorn for 2 minutes, or until the onion is soft. Remove and reserve. Clean the pan and add the remaining oil. When very hot, add the cold cooked rice and stir-fry for 3 minutes, or until it is heated through. Drizzle in the egg mixture and continue to stir-fry for 2–3 minutes until the egg has set. Add the prawns and crab meat, if using. Stir-fry for 1 minute. Season to taste with salt and pepper and add the sugar and soy sauce. Stir and spoon into a warmed serving dish. Garnish with a radish rose and chives. Serve immediately.

Keep any remaining rice in the refrigerator in a clean bowl covered with clingfilm for up to 2 days. I would not recommend freezing. Eat cold or, to reheat in the microwave, spoon onto a plate, cover with clingfilm and pierce 2–3 times. Heat on High for 2 minutes, allow to stand then eat. Ensure it is piping hot, if not, reheat for a further ½–1 minute.

TASTY TIP

For more flavour, cook the rice in a light unsalted chicken or vegetable stock.

Turkey Chow Mein

MAKES 2 PORTIONS

125 g/4 oz fine egg noodles
2 tbsp groundnut or
    vegetable oil
2 tsp light soy sauce
1 tbsp Chinese rice wine
    or malt vinegar
125 g/4 oz turkey steak,

cut into strips
1–2 garlic cloves, peeled and
    finely chopped
50 g/2 oz mangetout,
    finely sliced
50 g/2 oz cooked ham, cut
    into fine strips

2 tsp dark soy sauce
pinch sugar

To garnish (optional):
shredded spring onions
toasted sesame seeds

Place the egg noodles in a large bowl and cover with boiling water. Leave for 3–5 minutes, drain and add 1 teaspoon of the oil and stir lightly. Reserve. Place the light soy sauce, 1 tablespoon of the Chinese rice wine or vinegar and 1 teaspoon of the oil in a bowl. Add the turkey and stir well. Cover lightly and leave to marinate in the refrigerator for about 15 minutes. Heat the wok or large frying pan over a high heat, add 2 teaspoons of oil and, when very hot, add the turkey and its marinade and stir-fry for 2 minutes. Remove the turkey and juices and reserve. Wipe the wok or frying pan clean with absorbent kitchen paper.

Reheat the wok or frying pan and add 1 tablespoon of the oil. Add the garlic and toss in the oil for 20 seconds. Add the mangetout and the ham and stir-fry for 1 minute. Add the noodles, Chinese rice wine or vinegar, dark soy sauce and sugar. Season to taste with salt and pepper and stir-fry for 2 minutes. Add the turkey and juices and stir-fry for 4 minutes, or until the turkey is cooked. Garnish with spring onions and sesame seeds, if using, and serve.

This dish will not freeze well. Refrigerate in a clean dish and covered with clingfilm. Use the next day. It can be eaten hot or cold. To reheat, place 1–2 teaspoons oil in a frying pan and heat. When hot, add the chow mein and cook over a medium heat for 10–12 minutes until the turkey is piping hot. Stir frequently. Or, cover with clean clingfilm, pierce the top and heat on High for 2 minutes in the microwave. Allow to stand for 1 minute. Ensure that the turkey is piping hot.

Sweet & Sour Rice with Chicken

MAKES 2 PORTIONS

2 spring onions
1 tsp 1 tsp groundnut or olive oil
1 tsp Chinese five-spice powder
175 g /6 oz skinless chicken thighs or breast fillets

1 tbsp vegetable oil
1 garlic clove, peeled and crushed
1 small onion, peeled and sliced into thin wedges
125 g/4 oz white basmati rice
300 ml/½ pint water

2 tbsp tomato ketchup
1 tsp tomato purée
1 tbsp honey
2 tsp vinegar
2 tsp dark soy sauce
1 small carrot, peeled and cut into matchsticks

Trim the spring onions, then cut lengthways into fine strips. Drop into a bowl of iced water and reserve. Mix together the groundnut or olive oil and Chinese five-spice powder and use to rub into the chicken, then cut into small pieces. Heat a wok or large frying pan then add the vegetable oil and, when hot, cook the garlic and onion for 2–3 minutes until transparent and softened. Add the chicken to the wok or frying pan and stir-fry over a medium-high heat until the chicken is golden and cooked through. Using a slotted spoon, remove from the wok and keep warm.

Stir the rice into the wok or frying pan and add the water, tomato ketchup, tomato purée, honey, vinegar, soy sauce and carrot. Return the chicken to the wok or frying pan and stir. Bring to the boil, then simmer for 15 minutes or until almost all of the liquid is absorbed. Spoon into a warmed dish. Drain the spring onions and place on top, then serve immediately.

If wishing to keep, spoon into a clean bowl or dish and cover with clingfilm. Refrigerate for up to 2 days. To freeze, place the bowl or dish in a freezer bag, label and date. Use within 1 month and allow the chicken to thaw overnight in the refrigerator. To reheat, cover the top with clingfilm and pierce 2–3 times. Heat in the microwave for 2 minutes and allow to stand for 1 minute. If not piping hot, heat for a further 1 minute. It can also be heated on the hob. Heat 2 teaspoons of oil in a frying pan, add the rice and chicken, cover with a lid or kitchen foil and place over a low–medium heat. Stir occasionally, adding a little water or stock if the rice is becoming dry. Cook for 10–12 minutes until the chicken is thoroughly reheated and is piping hot.

FOOD FACT

Five-spice powder is a mixture of finely ground star anise, fennel, cinnamon, cloves and Szechuan pepper and adds a unique sweet and spicy aniseed flavour to food.

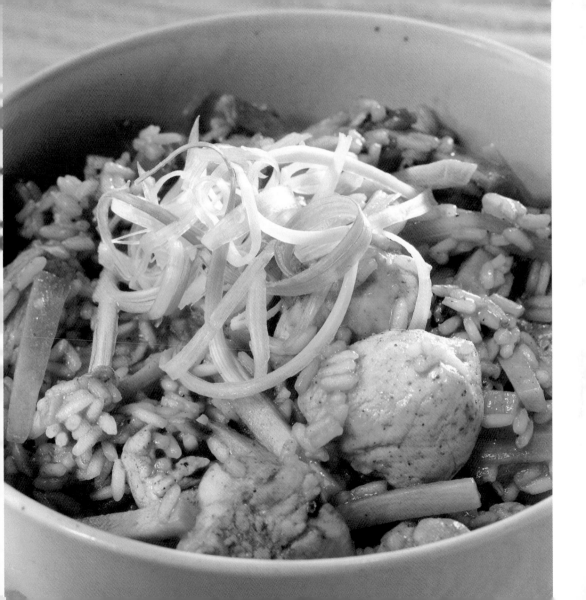

Warm Noodle Salad

MAKES 2 PORTIONS

40 g/1½ oz smooth
    peanut butter
1½ tbsp sesame or
    sunflower oil
2 tsp light soy sauce
1 tbsp vinegar
1 tsp freshly grated
    root ginger

125 g/4 oz Chinese fine
    egg noodles
25 g/1 oz beansprouts
50 g/2 oz baby sweetcorn
50 g/2 oz carrots, peeled and
    cut into matchsticks
50 g/2 oz mangetout

50 g/2 oz cucumber,
    cut into thin strips
2 spring onions, trimmed
    and finely shredded

Place the peanut butter, 1 tablespoon of the oil, the soy sauce, vinegar and ginger in a food processor or glass bowl. Blend until smooth, then stir in 2 tablespoons hot water and blend again until smooth, adding a little extra water if necessary. Pour the dressing into a jug and reserve.

Bring a saucepan of lightly salted water to the boil, add the noodles and beansprouts and cook for 4 minutes, or according to the packet instructions. Drain, rinse under cold running water and drain again. Stir in the remaining oil and keep warm.

Bring a saucepan of lightly salted water to the boil and add the baby sweetcorn, carrots and mangetout and cook for 3–4 minutes, or until just tender but still crisp. Drain and cut the mangetout in half. Slice the baby sweetcorn (if very large) into 2–3 pieces and arrange on a warmed serving dish with the noodles. Add the cucumber strips and spring onions. Spoon over a little of the dressing and serve immediately with the remaining dressing.

This dish is best eaten immediately but can be eaten cold. Keep covered with clingfilm in the refrigerator overnight and eat as a cold salad the next day. It would not freeze well.

FOOD FACT

There are 2 types of sesame oil. A light and pale one made from untoasted seeds; the other dark and rich. It has a strong nutty aroma and flavour, so choose a light version for this recipe.

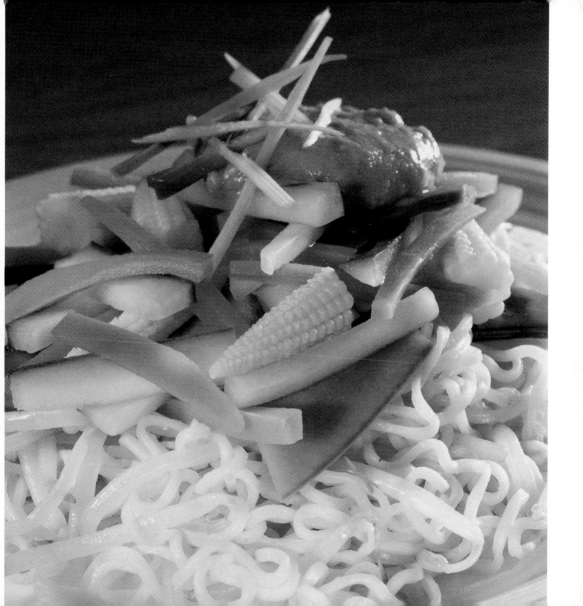

Honey Pork with Rice Noodles & Cashews

MAKES 2 LARGE PORTIONS

125 g/4 oz rice noodles
175 g/6 oz lean pork such as fillet
1 tbsp groundnut or vegetable oil
1 small onion, peeled and finely sliced into rings

1–2 garlic cloves, peeled and crushed
50 g/2 oz button mushrooms, halved
1–2 tbsp light soy sauce
1–2 tbsp clear honey
25 g/1 oz unsalted cashew nuts

½ red chilli, deseeded and finely chopped
2 spring onions, trimmed and finely chopped
freshly stir-fried vegetables, to serve

Soak the rice noodles in boiling water for 4 minutes, or according to packet instructions, then drain and reserve.

Trim and slice the pork into thin strips. Heat the wok or large frying pan, pour in the oil, and stir-fry the pork for 4–5 minutes, until cooked. Remove with a slotted spoon and keep warm.

Add the onion to the wok or frying pan and stir-fry gently for 2 minutes. Stir in the garlic and mushrooms and cook for a further 2 minutes, or until juices start to run from the mushrooms.

Blend the soy sauce with the honey then return the pork to the wok with this mixture. Add the cashew nuts and cook for 1–2 minutes, then add the rice noodles a little at a time. Stir-fry until everything is piping hot. Sprinkle with chopped chilli and spring onions. Serve immediately with freshly stir-fried vegetables.

This dish is best if eaten immediately; do not freeze. Either invite a friend round to share or store overnight covered with clingfilm and eat as a salad the next day.

TASTY TIP

In a hot wok, cook 1 chopped garlic clove and a little grated ginger in 1 tablespoon oil. Add a finely sliced pepper, some mangetout and spring onion. Stir-fry for 3–4 minutes. Serve with the pork.

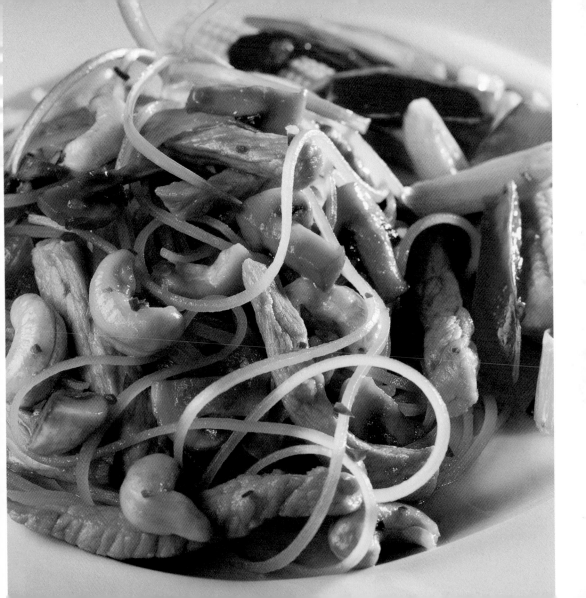

Chicken with Noodles

MAKES 2 LARGE PORTIONS

125 g/4 oz medium
   egg noodles
125 g/4 oz skinless, boneless
   chicken breast fillets
1 tbsp light soy sauce
2 tsp vinegar

5 tsp groundnut or
   vegetable oil
2 garlic cloves, peeled and
   finely chopped
50 g/2 oz mangetout

25 g/1 oz smoked back
   bacon, cut into fine strips
½ tsp sugar
2 spring onions, peeled
   and finely chopped
1 tsp sesame oil (optional)

Cook the noodles according to the packet instructions. Drain and refresh under cold water. Drain again and reserve.

Slice the chicken into fine shreds and mix with 2 teaspoons of the light soy sauce and vinegar. Leave to marinate in the refrigerator for 10 minutes.

Heat a wok or large frying pan, add 2 teaspoons of the oil and, when hot, stir-fry the chicken shreds for about 2 minutes, then transfer to a plate. Wipe the wok clean with absorbent kitchen paper.

Return the wok or frying pan to the heat and add the remaining oil. Add the garlic, then after 10 seconds add the mangetout and bacon. Stir-fry for a further 1 minute, then add the drained noodles, remaining soy sauce, sugar and spring onions. Stir-fry for a further 2 minutes, then add the reserved chicken.

FOOD FACT

Noodle dishes also make a
tasty salad if served cold.

Stir-fry for a further 3–4 minutes until the chicken is cooked through. Add the sesame oil, if using, and mix together. Serve either hot or cold.

This dish would keep overnight in the refrigerator, but do not freeze. Place in a bowl or dish and cover with clingfilm. Use the next day, cold.

Thai Coconut Chicken

MAKES 2 PORTIONS

½ tsp cumin seeds
½ tsp mustard seeds
½ tsp coriander seeds
½ tsp turmeric
1 bird's-eye chilli, deseeded
    and finely chopped
1 tbsp freshly grated
    root ginger

1 garlic clove, peeled and
    finely chopped
50 ml/2 fl oz double cream
2 skinless chicken thighs
2 tbsp groundnut or
    vegetable oil
1 medium onion, peeled and
    finely sliced

150 ml/¼ pint coconut milk
salt and freshly ground
    black pepper
2–4 tbsp chopped coriander
2 spring onions,
    shredded, to garnish
freshly cooked Thai fragrant
    rice, to serve

Heat the wok or large frying pan and add the cumin seeds, mustard seeds and coriander seeds. Dry-fry over a low to medium heat for 2 minutes, or until the fragrance becomes stronger and the seeds start to pop. Add the turmeric and leave to cool slightly. Grind the spices in a pestle and mortar, or a small grinder, to a fine powder.

Mix the chilli, ginger, garlic and the cream together in a small bowl, add the ground spices and mix. Place the chicken thighs in a shallow dish and spread the spice paste over the thighs. Heat the wok or large frying pan over a high heat, add the oil and, when hot, add the onion and stir-fry until golden brown. Add the chicken and the spice paste. Cook for 5–6 minutes, stirring occasionally, until evenly coloured. Add the coconut milk and season to taste with salt and pepper. Simmer the chicken for 15–20 minutes until the thighs are cooked through, taking care not to allow the mixture to boil. Stir in the chopped coriander and serve immediately with the freshly cooked rice, sprinkled with shredded spring onions.

TASTY TIP

Frying the spices before grinding them helps to release their essential oils. This, in turn, brings out the flavour of the spices, making them much more aromatic.

It is worth making double and freezing half. When cooked, cool the chicken to be frozen then place in a container with the sauce. Label and date, then freeze for up to 1 month. Allow to thaw completely in the refrigerator. It will also keep for 2–3 days in the refrigerator. To reheat, place in a frying pan with a lid or a medium-sized saucepan. Cook over a gentle heat for 10–12 minutes until piping hot. Add a little extra coconut milk if there is not much sauce.

Sausage & Bacon Risotto

MAKES 1 LARGE PORTION

75 g/3 oz long-grain rice
1 tsp olive or vegetable oil
25 g/1 oz butter, margarine or
  1 tablespoon oil
125 g/4 oz cocktail sausages
1 shallot, peeled and
  finely chopped

25 g/1 oz bacon lardons or
  thick slices of streaky
  bacon, chopped
50 g/2 oz chorizo or similar
  spicy sausage, cut into chunks
½ green pepper, deseeded
  and cut into strips

75 g canned sweetcorn,
  drained
1 tbsp freshly
  chopped parsley
25 g/1 oz mozzarella
  cheese, grated

Cook the rice in a saucepan of boiling salted water for 15 minutes or until tender, or according to packet instructions. Drain and rinse in cold water. Drain again and leave until completely cold.

Meanwhile, heat the wok or large frying pan, pour in the oil and melt the butter, margarine or add the extra oil, if using. Cook the cocktail sausages, turning continuously until cooked. Remove with a slotted spoon, cut in half and keep warm. Add the chopped shallot and bacon to the wok or frying pan and cook for 2–3 minutes until cooked but not browned. Add the spicy sausage and green pepper and stir-fry for a further 3 minutes. Add the cold rice and the sweetcorn to the wok or frying pan and stir-fry for 2 minutes, then return the cooked sausages to the wok or frying pan and stir over the heat until everything is piping hot. Garnish with the freshly chopped parsley and serve immediately with a little grated mozzarella cheese.

Leftovers will keep well in the refrigerator for up to 2 days. Spoon into a clean dish or bowl and cover with clingfilm. It will also freeze well. Place in a freezer bag, label and date. Keep for up to 1 month. Thaw in the refrigerator overnight. To reheat, stir the risotto and cover with clean clingfilm. Heat on High for 2 minutes, then allow to stand for 1 minute. Check it is piping hot; if not, reheat for an extra minute. Or, the risotto can be reheated in a saucepan. Pour a little oil into the pan, heat, then add the risotto. Cook over a gentle heat for 8–10 minutes, stirring frequently. Add a little water or stock if beginning to stick. Heat until piping hot.

Veggie Treats

Ratatouille

MAKES 1 LARGE PORTION

½ small red pepper
1 small courgette, trimmed
¼ small aubergine, trimmed
1 small onion, peeled

2 small ripe tomatoes
25 g/1 oz button
   mushrooms, wiped and
   halved or quartered

75 ml/3 fl oz tomato juice
1 tsp freshly chopped basil
salt and freshly ground
   black pepper

Deseed the pepper if necessary; remove the membrane with a small sharp knife and cut into small dice. Thickly slice the courgette and cut the aubergine into small dice. Slice the onion into rings.

Place the tomatoes in boiling water until their skins begin to peel away. Remove the skins from the tomatoes, cut into quarters and remove the seeds.

Place all the vegetables in a saucepan with the tomato juice and basil. Season to taste with salt and pepper. Bring to the boil, cover and simmer for 15 minutes or until the vegetables are tender. Remove the vegetables with a slotted spoon and arrange in a serving dish.

Bring the liquid in the pan to the boil and boil for 20 seconds until it is slightly thickened. Season the sauce to taste with salt and pepper. Pass the sauce through a sieve to remove some of the seeds and pour over the vegetables. Serve the ratatouille hot or cold.

Spoon any remaining ratatouille into a small bowl and cover with clingfilm. Keep in the refrigerator for up to 2 days. Do not freeze. The ratatouille can be reheated or eaten cold. If eating hot, spoon the ratatouille and its liquid into a small saucepan. Place over a gentle heat and bring to just below boiling point. Reduce the heat to a simmer and continue to heat for 5 minutes or until piping hot. Stir occasionally, adding a little extra tomato juice or water if becoming dry.

TASTY TIP

This dish would be perfect served as an accompaniment to a baked fish dish. It is also delicious in an omelette or as a jacket potato filling.

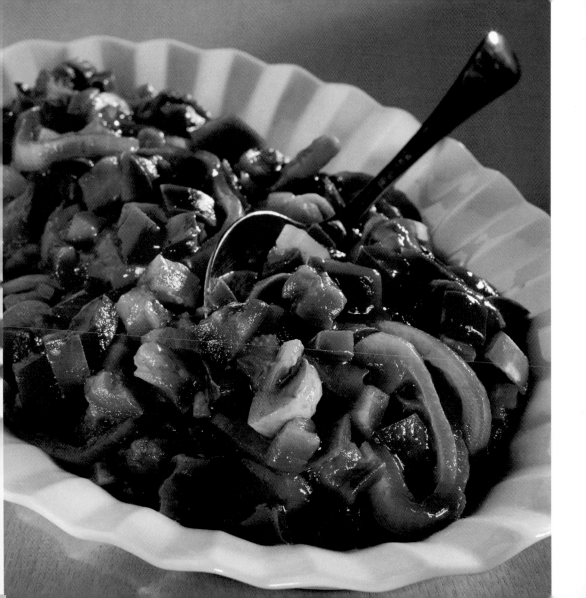

Rice–filled Peppers

MAKES 2 PORTIONS

3 ripe tomatoes
1 tbsp vegetable or olive oil
1 small onion, peeled
   and chopped
1 garlic clove, peeled
   and crushed

½ tsp sugar
50 g/2 oz cooked
   long-grain rice
25 g/1 oz pine nuts or
   chopped nuts, toasted
1 tsp freshly chopped oregano

salt and freshly ground
   black pepper
2 peppers

To serve:
mixed salad and crusty bread

Preheat the oven to 200°C/400°F/Gas Mark 6. Put the tomatoes in a small bowl and pour over boiling water to cover. Leave for 1 minute, then drain. Plunge the tomatoes into cold water to cool, then peel off the skins. Quarter, remove the seeds and chop.

Heat the oil in a frying pan and cook the onion gently for 10 minutes until softened. Add the garlic, chopped tomatoes and sugar. Gently cook for 10 minutes until thickened. Remove from the heat and stir the rice, nuts and oregano into the sauce. Season to taste with salt and pepper.

Halve the peppers lengthways, cutting through and leaving the stem on. Remove the seeds and cores, then put the peppers in a lightly oiled roasting tin, cut-side down, and cook in the preheated oven for about 10 minutes. Turn the peppers so they are cut-side up. Spoon in the filling, then cover with kitchen foil. Return to the oven for 15 minutes, or until the peppers are very tender, removing the foil for the last 5 minutes to allow the tops to brown a little. Serve with a mixed salad and plenty of warm, crusty bread.

Any remaining peppers will keep well in the refrigerator for up to 2 days. Place in a clean dish and cover with clingfilm. Eat hot or cold. They would not freeze very well. To reheat, pierce the clingfilm and heat in the microwave on High for 2 minutes. Allow to stand for 1 minute before eating. Or, heat the oven to 180°C/350°F/Gas Mark 4. Place the peppers in an ovenproof dish and pour a little water around the base. Cover with kitchen foil. Heat for 15–20 minutes until piping hot.

HELPFUL HINT

You may need to take a very thin slice from the bottom of the peppers so they can stand on the baking sheet. Take care not to cut right through.

Vegetable & Lentil Casserole

MAKES 1 LARGE PORTION

125 g/4 oz puy lentils

1–2 tbsp vegetable or olive oil

1 small onion, peeled and chopped

2 garlic cloves, peeled and crushed

150 g/5 oz carrots, peeled and sliced into chunks

1 celery stalk, trimmed and sliced

175 g/6 oz butternut squash, peeled, seeds removed and diced

450 ml/¾ pint vegetable stock

salt and freshly ground black pepper

few fresh oregano sprigs, plus extra to garnish

1 small red pepper, deseeded and chopped

1 small courgette, trimmed and sliced

2–3 tbsp natural yogurt or sour cream, to serve

Preheat the oven to 160°C/325°F/Gas Mark 3. Pour the lentils out onto a plate and look through them for any small stones, then rinse the lentils and reserve. Heat the oil in a large ovenproof casserole (or a deep frying pan); add the onion, garlic, carrots and celery and sauté for 5 minutes, stirring occasionally. Add the squash and lentils. Pour in the stock and season to taste with salt and pepper. Add the oregano sprigs and bring to the boil.

If a frying pan has been used, transfer everything to a casserole. Cover with a lid and cook in the oven for 25 minutes. Remove from the oven; add the red pepper and courgette and stir. Return the casserole to the oven and cook for a further 20 minutes, or until all the vegetables are tender. Adjust the seasoning, garnish with oregano sprigs and serve with sour cream on the side.

This will keep well in the refrigerator for up to 3 days. Spoon any remaining casserole into a dish and cover with clingfilm. To reheat, place in an ovenproof dish and add a little extra stock if looking a little dry. Cover with kitchen foil and heat at 180°C/350°F/Gas Mark 4 for 20 minutes or until piping hot. Stir once or twice during reheating. Or, reheat in the microwave. Place the casserole in a microwavable dish and cover with clingfilm. Pierce the film 2–3 times. Heat on High for 3 minutes then stir and allow to stand for 1 minute before eating.

TASTY TIP

Other vegetables can be added to the casserole, such as sweet potato, aubergine, turnips or parsnips.

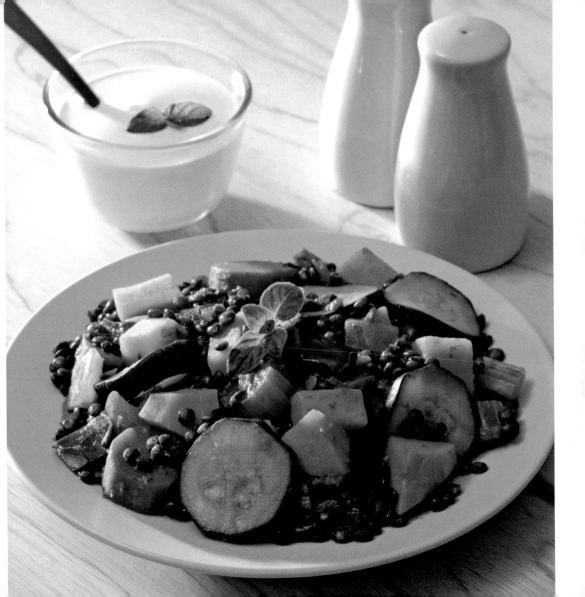

Vegetarian
Spaghetti Bolognese

MAKES 2 PORTIONS

1 tbsp vegetable or olive oil
1 small onion, peeled and
    finely chopped
1 small carrot, peeled and
    finely chopped
1 small celery stalk, trimmed
    and finely chopped

175 g/6 oz Quorn mince
200 ml/7 fl oz
    vegetable stock
1–2 tbsp tomato purée
75 g/3 oz spaghetti
4 tbsp natural Greek yogurt

salt and freshly ground
    black pepper
1 tsp freshly chopped
    parsley

Heat the oil in a large saucepan and add the onion, carrot and celery. Cook gently for 5 minutes, until softened and starting to brown. Add the Quorn mince and cook a further 2–3 minutes.

Add half the stock to the Quorn mixture along with the tomato purée. Cover and simmer gently for about 15 minutes, adding the remaining stock as necessary.

Meanwhile, bring a large pan of salted water to the boil and add the spaghetti. Cook until *al dente* or according to the packet instructions. Drain well. Remove the sauce from the heat, add the yogurt and season to taste with salt and pepper. Stir in the parsley and serve immediately with the pasta.

The sauce will keep well in the refrigerator for up to 3 days. Spoon into a dish and cover with clingfilm. I would not recommend keeping the spaghetti; cook this fresh as required. You could freeze the sauce for up to 1 month. Thaw before using.

To reheat, place the Bolognese sauce in a saucepan over a gentle heat. Add a little extra stock. Bring slowly to the boil and simmer for 5–8 minutes, stirring occasionally, until piping hot.

HELPFUL HINT

Quorn is a mycroprotein that is derived from the mushroom family. An equivalent amount of soya mince can be used in this recipe.

Baby Onion Risotto

MAKES 2 PORTIONS

For the baby onions:
1 tbsp vegetable or olive oil
175 g/6 oz baby onions,
    peeled and halved if large
pinch of sugar
1 tsp freshly chopped thyme

For the risotto:
1 tbsp vegetable or olive oil
1 small onion, peeled and
    finely chopped
2 garlic cloves, peeled and
    finely chopped
175 g/6 oz risotto rice
600 ml/1 pint hot
    vegetable stock

50 g/2 oz low-fat soft
    goat's cheese
salt and freshly ground
    black pepper
fresh thyme sprigs,
    to garnish
rocket leaves, to serve
    (optional)

For the onions, heat the oil in a saucepan and add the onions and sugar. Cover and cook over a low heat, stirring occasionally, for 20–25 minutes until caramelised. Uncover during the last 10 minutes. Meanwhile, for the risotto, heat the oil in a large frying pan and add the chopped onion. Cook over a medium heat for 5 minutes until softened. Add the garlic and cook for a further 30 seconds. Add the rice and stir well. Add the stock a ladleful at a time, stirring well and waiting until the last ladleful has been absorbed before stirring in the next. It will take 20–25 minutes to add all the stock; the rice should be just cooked but still firm. Remove from the heat.

Add the thyme to the onions and cook briefly. Increase the heat and allow the mixture to bubble for 2–3 minutes until almost evaporated. Add the onions to the risotto along with the goat's cheese. Stir well and season to taste with salt and pepper. Garnish with sprigs of fresh thyme. Serve immediately with the rocket leaves, if using.

This will keep well in the refrigerator for up to 2 days. Spoon into a dish and cover with clingfilm. I would not recommend freezing. To reheat, place in a saucepan over a gentle heat, add a little extra stock, bring slowly to the boil and simmer for 5–8 minutes, stirring occasionally, until piping hot. Or, reheat in the microwave. Spoon into a microwaveable dish or plate, cover with clingfilm, pierce 2–3 times and heat on High for 2 minutes. Allow to stand for 1 minute before eating.

HELPFUL HINT

To peel baby onions, put into a saucepan of water and bring to the boil. Drain and run under cold water. The skins will loosen and peel easily.

Boston-style Baked Beans

MAKES 1 LARGE PORTION

125 g/4 oz mixed dried pulses,
  e.g. haricot, flageolet,
  cannellini, chickpeas, pinto
1 small onion, peeled and
  finely chopped
1–2 tbsp black treacle
1–2 tbsp mustard
2 tsp light brown soft sugar

salt and freshly ground pepper

**For the corn bread
  (optional):**
125 g/4 oz plain flour
150 g/5 oz fine cornmeal
2 tbsp caster sugar
2½ tsp baking powder

½ tsp salt
2 tbsp freshly
  chopped thyme
2 medium eggs
200 ml/7 fl oz milk
2 tbsp melted margarine
  or butter
parsley sprig, to garnish

Preheat the oven to 130°C/250°F/Gas Mark ½. Put the pulses into a large saucepan and cover with twice their volume of water. Bring to the boil and simmer for 2 minutes. Leave to stand for 1 hour. Return to the boil and boil rapidly for about 10 minutes. Drain and reserve. Mix together the onion, treacle, mustard and sugar. Add the drained beans and 300 ml/½ pint fresh water. Stir well, bring to the boil, cover and transfer to the oven for 4 hours in an ovenproof dish, stirring hourly and adding more water if necessary. When they are cooked, remove from the oven and keep warm. Increase the temperature to 200°C/400°F/Gas Mark 6.

To make the corn bread, mix together the flour, cornmeal, sugar, baking powder, salt and three-quarters of the thyme. In a separate bowl, beat the eggs, then stir in the milk and butter. Pour the wet ingredients onto the dry and stir to combine. Pour into a buttered 18 cm/7 inch square tin. Sprinkle over the remaining thyme. Bake for 30 minutes until golden and risen or a toothpick inserted into the centre comes out clean. Reheat the beans. Season and serve immediately, garnished with a parsley sprig and served with squares of corn bread.

Keep leftover beans for up to 4 days in the refrigerator covered with clingfilm. Keep the corn bread wrapped in foil in a bread bin or the refrigerator. Warm in the microwave for 1 minute. To reheat the beans, heat gently in a saucepan with a little stock or water. Bring to the boil, reduce to a simmer, stir and cover. Cook for 5–8 minutes, stirring occasionally. Eat when piping hot.

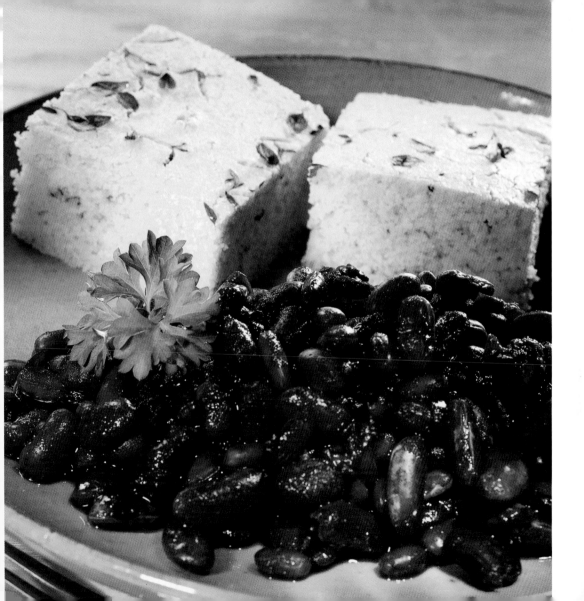

Roasted Butternut Squash

MAKES 2 LARGE PORTIONS

1 small butternut squash
2 garlic cloves, peeled
    and crushed
2 tbsp vegetable or olive oil
salt and freshly ground
    black pepper
1 medium-sized leek,
    trimmed, cleaned and
    thinly sliced

200 g/7 oz canned cannellini
    beans, drained and rinsed
    (or use 75 g/3 oz dried
    beans – see Helpful Hint)
25 g/1 oz fine French
    beans, halved
150 ml/¼ pint vegetable stock
25 g/1 oz rocket
    or watercress

2 tsp freshly snipped chives
fresh chives, to garnish
    (optional)

To serve:
4 tbsp natural or
    Greek yogurt
mixed salad

HELPFUL HINT

Soak dried beans in water overnight. Drain and boil rapidly in fresh water for 10 minutes, then simmer gently for 45–50 minutes until tender.

Preheat the oven to 200°C/400°F/Gas Mark 6. Cut the butternut squash in half lengthwise and scoop out all of the seeds. Score the squash in a diamond pattern with a sharp knife. Mix the garlic with one tablespoon of the oil and brush over the cut surfaces of the squash. Season well with salt and pepper. Put on a baking sheet and roast for 40 minutes until tender.

Heat the remaining oil in a saucepan and fry the leeks for 5 minutes. Add the drained cannellini beans, French beans and vegetable stock. Bring to the boil and simmer gently for 5 minutes until the French beans are tender. Remove from the heat and stir in the rocket or watercress and chives. Season well. Remove the squash from the oven and allow to cool for 5 minutes. Spoon in the bean mixture. Garnish with a few snipped chives, if using, and serve immediately with the yogurt and a mixed salad.

The squash will keep well in the refrigerator for up to 2 days. Place on a plate and cover with clingfilm. I would not recommend freezing. To reheat, place the squash in a roasting tin and pour round a little water. Cover with kitchen foil and reheat in an oven preheated to 180°C/350°F/Gas Mark 4 for 15–20 minutes until piping hot. Or, it can be reheated in the microwave. Place on a microwaveable dish or plate and cover with clingfilm. Pierce 2–3 times, heat on High for 2 minutes 30 seconds and allow to stand for 1 minute before eating.

Vegetarian Cassoulet

MAKES 2 LARGE PORTIONS

125 g/4 oz dried haricot
   beans, soaked overnight
1 medium onion
1 bay leaf
750 ml/1¼ pints cold water
350 g/12 oz potatoes,
   peeled and cut into
   1 cm/½ inch slices
salt and freshly ground

black pepper
3 tsp vegetable or olive oil
1 large garlic clove, peeled
   and crushed
1 leek, trimmed and sliced
200 g can chopped tomatoes
1 tsp sugar
1–2 tsp freshly chopped thyme
1–2 tsp freshly

chopped parsley
1 courgette, trimmed
   and sliced

For the topping:
50 g/2 oz fresh white
   breadcrumbs
25 g/1oz Cheddar cheese,
   finely grated

HELPFUL HINT

Try using a small can of mixed beans with a small can of butter beans. This will speed up everything, as there is no need to soak or cook the beans first – just drain, rinse and use.

Preheat the oven to 180°C/350°F/Gas Mark 4, 10 minutes before required. Drain the beans, rinse under cold water and put in a saucepan. Peel the onion and add half to the beans with the bay leaf. Pour in the water. Bring to a rapid boil and cook for 10 minutes, then turn down the heat, cover and simmer for 50 minutes, or until the beans are almost tender. Drain, reserving the liquor, but discarding the onion and bay leaf. Cook the potatoes in a saucepan of lightly salted boiling water for 6–7 minutes until almost tender. Drain and reserve.

Peel and chop the remaining half of onion. Heat the oil in a frying pan and cook the onion with the garlic and leek for 10 minutes until softened. Stir in the tomatoes, sugar, thyme and parsley. Stir in the beans, with 200 ml/7 fl oz of the reserved liquor and season to taste. Simmer, uncovered, for 5 minutes. Layer the potato and courgette slices and ladlefuls of the bean mixture in a large flameproof casserole. To make the topping, mix together the breadcrumbs and cheese and sprinkle over the top. Bake in the preheated oven for 40 minutes, or until the vegetables are cooked through and the topping is golden brown and crisp. Serve immediately.

Spoon leftovers into a dish or container and cover with clingfilm or a lid and keep in the refrigerator for up to 3 days. Reheat gently in a saucepan, with a little stock or water if dry. Bring to the boil, reduce to a simmer and cook for 10 minutes or until piping hot. Stir occasionally.

Bulgur Wheat Salad with Minty Lemon Dressing

MAKES 1 LARGE PORTION

50 g/2 oz bulgur wheat
5 cm/2 inch piece cucumber
2 shallots, peeled
50 g/2 oz baby sweetcorn
3 ripe but firm
   cherry tomatoes

For the dressing:
1 tbsp grated lemon zest
2 tbsp lemon juice
1 tbsp freshly chopped mint
2 tsp freshly
   chopped parsley

1–2 tsp clear honey
2 tbsp vegetable or
   sunflower oil
salt and freshly ground
   black pepper

Place the bulgur wheat in a saucepan and cover with boiling water.

Simmer for about 10 minutes, then drain thoroughly and turn into a serving bowl.

Cut the cucumber into small dice, chop the shallots finely and reserve. Steam the sweetcorn over a pan of boiling water for 10 minutes or until tender. Drain and slice into thick chunks.

Cut a cross on the top of each tomato and place in boiling water until their skins start to peel away. Remove the skins and the seeds and cut the tomatoes into small dice.

Make the dressing by briskly whisking all the ingredients in a small bowl until mixed well.

When the bulgur wheat has cooled a little, add all the prepared vegetables and stir in the dressing. Season to taste with salt and pepper and serve.

Any remaining salad can be kept in the refrigerator. Spoon into a clean bowl, cover with clingfilm and keep for up to 2 days. Stir before eating. Not suitable for freezing.

TASTY TIP

Other ingredients can be added if liked. Try 25 g/1 oz raisins or dried chopped apricots. Canned chick peas would be good, as would a sprinkling of ground cinnamon.

FOOD FACT

This dish is loosely based on the Middle Eastern dish tabbouleh, a type of salad in which all the ingredients are mixed together and served cold.

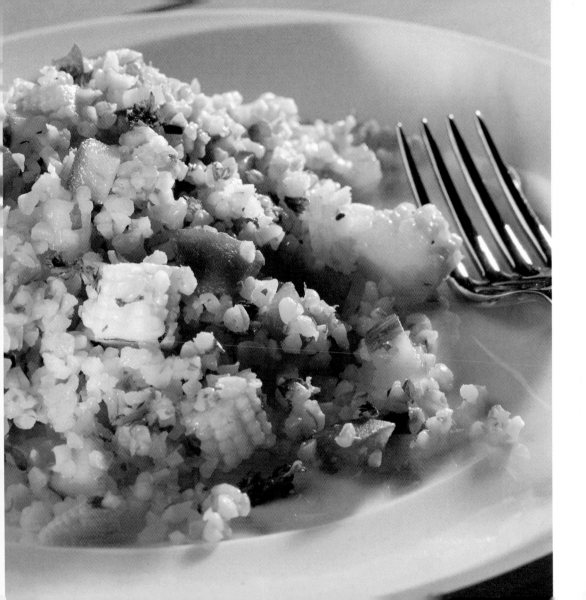

Three Bean Tagine

MAKES 1 LARGE PORTION

few saffron strands or
½ tsp turmeric
2 tbsp vegetable or olive oil
1 small aubergine, trimmed
and diced
1 small onion, peeled
and chopped
125 g/4 oz sweet potatoes,
peeled and diced

1 medium carrot, peeled and
chopped
1 cinnamon stick, bruised, or
½–1 tsp ground cinnamon
½ tsp ground cumin
salt and freshly ground
black pepper
300 ml/½ pint vegetable stock
2 fresh mint sprigs

75 g/3 oz canned red kidney
beans, drained
50 g/2 oz canned haricot
beans, drained
50 g/2 oz canned flageolet
beans, drained
50 g/2 oz ready-to-eat dried
apricots, chopped
1 tsp freshly chopped mint,
to garnish

Place warm water into a small bowl and sprinkle with saffron strands, if using. Leave to infuse for at least 10 minutes.

Heat the oil in a large, heavy-based saucepan, add the aubergine and onion and fry for 5 minutes before adding the sweet potatoes, carrot, cinnamon stick or ground cinnamon, turmeric, if using, and ground cumin. Cook, stirring, until the vegetables are lightly coated in the spices. Add the saffron with the soaking liquid, if using, and season to taste with salt and pepper. Pour in the stock and add the mint sprigs.

Rinse the beans, add to the pan and bring to the boil. Reduce the heat, cover with a lid and simmer for 20 minutes. Add the apricots and cook, stirring occasionally, for a further 10 minutes or until the vegetables are tender. Adjust the seasoning to taste, then serve sprinkled with chopped mint.

Any remaining tagine can be kept in the refrigerator. Spoon into a small bowl or container and cover with either clingfilm or a lid. Keep for up to 2 days. Stir before eating. Do not freeze the tagine or reheat.

Sicilian Baked Aubergine

MAKES 1 LARGE PORTION

1 small aubergine, trimmed
1 celery stalk, trimmed
1 large ripe tomato
1 tsp vegetable or
   sunflower oil
2 shallots, peeled and
   finely chopped

1½ tsp tomato purée
15 g/½ oz green pitted
   olives (optional)
15 g/½ oz black pitted
   olives (optional)
salt and freshly ground
   black pepper

1 tbsp vinegar or lemon juice
1 tsp caster sugar
1 tsp freshly chopped basil,
   to garnish
mixed salad leaves,
   to serve

Preheat the oven to 200°C/400°F/Gas Mark 6. Cut the aubergine into small cubes and place on an oiled baking tray. Cover the tray with kitchen foil and bake in the preheated oven for 15–20 minutes until soft. Reserve, to allow the aubergine to cool.

Place the celery and tomato in a large bowl and cover with boiling water. Remove the tomato from the bowl when the skin begins to peel away and remove the skins. Deseed and chop the flesh into small pieces. Remove the celery from the bowl of water, finely chop and reserve.

Pour the oil into a nonstick saucepan; add the chopped shallots and fry gently for 2–3 minutes until soft. Add the celery, tomato, tomato purée and olives, if using. Season to taste with salt and pepper. Simmer gently for 3–4 minutes. Add the vinegar or lemon juice, sugar and cooled aubergine to the pan and heat gently for 2–3 minutes until all the ingredients are well blended. Reserve to allow the aubergine mixture to cool. When cool, garnish with the chopped basil and serve cold with salad leaves.

Any remaining aubergine can be eaten the next day. Spoon into a bowl or container and cover with either clingfilm or lid. Keep in the refrigerator overnight. Stir before eating. Do not freeze.

Chargrilled Vegetable & Goats' Cheese Pizza

MAKES 1 LARGE PORTION

1 bought 23–30 cm/
  10–12 inch pizza base

For the topping:
1 small aubergine,
  thinly sliced
1 small courgette trimmed
  and sliced lengthways

½ yellow pepper, deseeded
  and cut in half
1 small red onion, peeled
  and sliced into very
  thin wedges
2 tbsp vegetable or olive oil
50 g/2 oz cooked new
  potatoes, halved

200 g/7 oz canned tomatoes,
  chopped and drained
1 tsp freshly chopped
  oregano
50 g/2 oz goats' cheese,
  crumbled

Preheat the oven to 220°C/425°F/Gas Mark 7, 15 minutes before using. Put a baking sheet in the oven to heat up, 5 minutes before baking the pizza. Line a grill rack with kitchen foil.

To make the topping, arrange the aubergine, courgette, pepper and onion, skin-side up, on the grill rack and brush with 1 tablespoon of the oil. Grill for 4–5 minutes. Turn the vegetables and brush with the remaining oil. Grill for 3–4 minutes. Cool, skin and slice the pepper. Put all of the vegetables in a bowl, add the halved new potatoes and toss gently together. Set aside.

Mix the tomatoes and oregano together and spread over the pizza base. Put the pizza on the preheated baking sheet and bake for 8 minutes.

Arrange the vegetables and goats' cheese on top and bake for 8–10 minutes. Serve.

The pizza needs to be eaten immediately and does not keep successfully.

HELPFUL HINT

It would be a good idea to have a few pizza bases in the freezer so that a quick supper can be made. The pizza bases are normally sold in packs of 2. Freeze separately.

Calypso Rice with Curried Bananas

MAKES 1 LARGE PORTION

1 tbsp vegetable or
  sunflower oil
1 small onion, peeled
  and finely chopped
1 garlic clove, peeled
  and crushed
½–1 red chilli, deseeded
  and finely chopped
½ red pepper, deseeded
  and chopped

50 g/2 oz basmati rice
juice of ½ lemon
125–150 ml/4–5 fl oz
  vegetable stock
75 g/3oz canned black-eye
  beans, drained and rinsed
1 tsp freshly chopped parsley
salt and freshly ground
  black pepper
coriander sprigs, to garnish

For the bananas (optional):
1–2, depending on size,
  green bananas
1–2 tbsp vegetable or
  sunflower oil
75 ml/3 fl oz coconut milk
2 tsp mild curry paste

Heat the oil in a large frying pan and gently cook the onion, for 5–8 minutes until soft. Add the garlic, chilli and red pepper and cook for 2–3 minutes. Rinse the rice under cold water, then add to the pan and stir. Pour in the lemon juice and 125 ml/4 fl oz of stock, bring to the boil, cover and simmer. Cook for 12–15 minutes until the rice is tender and the stock is absorbed; add the remaining stock if necessary. Stir in the black-eye beans and parsley and season to taste with salt and pepper. Leave to stand, covered, for 5 minutes before serving.

While the rice is cooking, make the curried green bananas, if using. Remove the skins from the bananas – they may need to be cut off with a sharp knife. Slice the flesh thickly. Heat the oil in a frying pan and cook the bananas, for 2–3 minutes, or until lightly browned. Pour the coconut milk into the pan and stir in the curry paste. Add the banana slices to the coconut milk and simmer, uncovered, over a low heat for 8–10 minutes, or until the bananas are very soft and the coconut milk slightly reduced. Spoon the rice onto warmed serving plates, garnish with coriander and serve immediately with the curried bananas.

Any remaining rice and bananas can be kept overnight in the refrigerator. Spoon into a clean bowl and cover with clingfilm. Next day either eat cold or heat on High for 2 minutes in the microwave.

Aduki Bean & Rice Burgers

MAKES 2 PORTIONS

2 tbsp vegetable or
   sunflower oil
1 small onion, peeled and
   very finely chopped
1 garlic clove, peeled
   and crushed
1 tsp curry paste
125 g/4 oz basmati rice
200 g/7 oz canned aduki
   beans, drained and rinsed

125 ml/4 fl oz vegetable stock
50 g/2 oz firm tofu, crumbled
1 tbsp freshly
   chopped coriander
salt and freshly ground
   black pepper

For the carrot raita:
1 small carrot, peeled
   and grated

¼ cucumber, cut into
   tiny dice
50 ml/2 fl oz Greek yogurt

To serve:
wholemeal baps
tomato slices
lettuce leaves

Heat 1 tablespoon of the oil in a saucepan and gently cook the onion for 5–8 minutes until soft. Add the garlic and curry paste and cook for a few more seconds. Stir in the rice and beans. Pour in the stock, bring to the boil and simmer for 12 minutes, or until all the stock has been absorbed – do not lift the lid for the first 10 minutes of cooking. Reserve.

Lightly mash the tofu. Add to the rice mixture with the coriander, salt and pepper. Mix. Divide the mixture into 4 and shape into burgers. Chill in the refrigerator for 30 minutes. Meanwhile, make the raita. Mix together the carrot, cucumber and Greek yogurt. Spoon into a small bowl and chill in the refrigerator until ready to serve.

FOOD FACT

Firm tofu is sold in blocks.
It is made in a similar way
to soft cheese and
is the pressed curds of
soya milk.

Heat the remaining oil in a large frying pan. Fry the burgers for 4–5 minutes on each side, or until lightly browned. Serve in the baps with tomato slices and lettuce. Accompany with the raita.

If wishing to eat two of the burgers the next day, shape but do not fry. Place on a plate, cover with clingfilm and refrigerate. They will also feeze, if liked. Wrap in kitchen foil, label and date. Keep for up to 1 month. Thaw before cooking. In either case, cook as above when required.

Black Bean Chilli

MAKES 1 LARGE PORTION

75 g/3 oz black beans and black-eye beans, soaked overnight
1 tbsp vegetable or olive oil
1 small onion, peeled and finely chopped
½ red pepper, deseeded and diced
1 garlic clove, peeled and finely chopped
½–1 red chilli, deseeded and finely chopped (optional)
1 tsp chilli powder
½ tsp ground cumin
1 tsp ground coriander
150 g/5 oz canned tomatoes, chopped
300 ml/½ pint vegetable stock

salt and freshly ground black pepper

To serve:
chunky guacamole or avocado salsa (optional)
low-fat natural yogurt
lime or lemon slices (optional)
coriander sprigs

Drain the beans and place in a medium saucepan with at least twice their volume of fresh water. Bring slowly to the boil, skimming off any froth that rises to the surface. Boil rapidly for 10 minutes, then reduce the heat and simmer for about 45 minutes, adding more water if necessary. Drain and reserve.

Heat the oil in a medium saucepan and add the onion and pepper. Cook for 3–4 minutes until softened. Add the garlic and chilli, if using. Cook for 5 minutes, or until the onion and pepper have softened. Add the chilli powder, cumin and coriander and cook for 30 seconds. Add the beans along with the canned tomatoes, stock and seasoning to taste. Bring to the boil and simmer uncovered for 40–45 minutes until the beans and vegetables are tender and the sauce has reduced. Stir occasionally and add a little extra stock if becoming too dry. Remove the chilli from the heat. Leave for 2 minutes. Stir well. Serve with the chunky guacamole or avocado salsa, if using, yogurt, lemon or lime wedges, if using, and coriander.

The chilli will intensify with keeping. Place any remaining in a bowl and cover with clingfilm. Keep in the refrigerator for up to 3 days. If liked, it can be frozen. Spoon into a container or freezer bag, label and date. Keep for up to 1 month. Thaw in the refrigerator. Reheat in a pan over a gentle heat for 10–12 minutes. Add a little extra stock or water and stir occasionally.

Marinated Vegetable Kebabs

MAKES 4 KEBABS

1 small courgette cut into
  2 cm/¾ inch pieces
¼ green pepper, deseeded
  and cut into 2.5 cm/
  1 inch pieces
¼ red pepper, deseeded
  and cut into 2.5 cm/
  1 inch pieces
¼ yellow pepper, deseeded

and cut into 2.5 cm/
  1 inch pieces
4 baby onions, peeled
4 button mushrooms
4 cherry tomatoes
freshly chopped parsley,
  to garnish
freshly cooked couscous,
  to serve (optional)

For the marinade:
1 tbsp vegetable or light
  olive oil
2 tbsp light soy sauce
1 red chilli, deseeded
  and finely chopped
2 garlic cloves, peeled
  and crushed

Place the courgette, peppers and baby onions in a pan of just boiled water. Bring back to the boil and simmer for about 30 seconds. Drain and rinse the vegetables in cold water and dry on absorbent kitchen paper.

Thread the cooked vegetables and the mushrooms and tomatoes alternately onto skewers and place in a large shallow dish.

Make the marinade by whisking all the ingredients together until thoroughly blended. Pour the marinade evenly over the kebabs, then chill in the refrigerator for at least 1 hour. Spoon the marinade over the kebabs occasionally during this time.

HELPFUL HINT

If using wooden skewers
and cooking over a
barbecue, soak in cold
water for 30 minutes
before using.

Place the kebabs in a hot griddle pan or on a hot barbecue and cook gently for 10–12 minutes. Turn the kebabs frequently and brush with the marinade when needed. When the vegetables are tender, sprinkle over the chopped parsley and serve immediately with couscous, if using.

Any prepared but uncooked kebabs that you are not going to eat can be kept overnight in the refrigerator. Next day cook as above.

Hearty Meals

Chilli Con Carne with Crispy–skinned Potato

MAKES 1 LARGE PORTION

1 tbsp vegetable or
   sunflower oil, plus
   extra for brushing
1 small onion, peeled
   and finely chopped
1 garlic clove, peeled
   and finely chopped
½–1 red chilli, deseeded and
   finely chopped (optional)

175 g/6 oz lean beef mince
1–2 tsp, depending on heat
   tolerance, chilli powder
200 g/7 oz canned
   tomatoes, chopped
2 tsp tomato purée
100 g/3½ oz canned red
   kidney beans, drained
   and rinsed

1 large baking potato
coarse salt and freshly
   ground black pepper

To serve:
ready-made guacamole
   (optional)
Greek yogurt or
   natural yogurt

Preheat the oven to 150°C/300°F/Gas Mark 2. Heat the oil in a flameproof casserole and add the onion. Cook gently for 5–8 minutes until soft and lightly browned. Add the garlic and chilli, if using, and cook briefly. Increase the heat. Add the lean mince and cook for a further 5 minutes, stirring occasionally, until browned. Add the chilli powder and stir well. Cook for about 2 minutes, then add the chopped tomatoes and tomato purée. Bring slowly to the boil. Cover and cook in the preheated oven for 1½ hours. Remove from the oven and stir in the kidney beans. Return to the oven for a further 15 minutes. Meanwhile, brush a little vegetable oil all over the potato and rub on some coarse salt. Put the potato in the oven alongside the chilli.

Remove the chilli and potato from the oven. Cut a cross in the potato, and then squeeze to open slightly and season to taste with salt and pepper. Serve with the chilli, guacamole and yogurt.

Keep any remaining cooked chilli in a clean bowl covered with clingfilm in the refrigerator for up to 2 days. Or, place in a freezer bag, label and date. Freeze for up to 2 weeks and thaw in the refrigerator for at least 8 hours. To reheat, spoon into a small saucepan, place over a gentle heat on the hob and cook, stirring, for 8–10 minutes, adding a little extra stock or water if looking dry. Or, heat in a small bowl covered with clingfilm and pierced 2–3 times on High in the microwave for 2 minutes. Stand for 1 minute, then stir before eating. Serve with freshly cooked rice.

TASTY TIP
If liked, the chilli can be cooked on the hob instead of the oven, for 30–35 minutes, and the potato cooked in the microwave for 4–5 minutes depending on size.

Pork Sausages with Onion Gravy & Best–ever Mash

MAKES 2 LARGE PORTIONS

1 tbsp vegetable or olive oil
1 medium onion, peeled
   and thinly sliced
pinch sugar
1 tsp freshly chopped thyme
   or use ½ tsp dried thyme
1 tsp plain flour

150 ml/¼ pint
   vegetable stock
6 pork sausages

For the mash:
225 g/8 oz floury
   potatoes, peeled
2 tsp margarine or butter
2 tbsp natural yogurt or milk
salt and freshly ground
   black pepper

Heat the oil and add the onion. Cover and cook gently for about 12 minutes until the onion has collapsed. Add the sugar and stir well. Uncover and continue to cook, stirring often, until the onion is very soft and golden. Add the thyme, stir well, then add the flour, stirring. Gradually add the stock. Bring to the boil and simmer gently for 10 minutes.

Meanwhile, put the sausages in a frying pan and cook over a medium heat for about 15–20 minutes, turning often, until golden brown and slightly sticky all over.

For the mash, boil the potatoes in plenty of lightly salted water for 15–18 minutes until tender. Drain well and return to the saucepan. Put the saucepan over a low heat to allow the potatoes to dry thoroughly. Remove from the heat and add the margarine or butter, yogurt or milk and salt and pepper. Mash thoroughly. Serve the potato mash with the sausages and onion gravy.

HELPFUL HINT

Sausages should always be cooked slowly over a gentle heat to ensure that they are cooked through.

Place any remaining sausages and mash on a plate or in a dish, cover with clingfilm and keep overnight in the refrigerator. Pour any gravy into a small jug and cover with clingfilm. Do not freeze. To reheat, pierce the clingfilm covering the sausages and mash in 2–3 places. Heat on High in the microwave for 2 minutes 20 seconds. Allow to stand for 1 minute. If not piping hot, heat for a further minute. Stand for 1 more minute then eat. Pour the gravy into a small saucepan and heat, stirring until it comes to the boil. Add a little extra stock if necessary.

Creamy Chicken Stroganoff

MAKES 1 LARGE PORTION

125 g/4 oz skinless chicken
    breast fillets
2 tsp vegetable or
    sunflower oil
2 tsp margarine or butter
1 small onion, peeled
    and sliced

50 g/2 oz chestnut
    mushrooms, wiped
    and sliced
1 tsp freshly chopped thyme
    or ½ tsp dried thyme
50 ml/2 fl oz chicken stock
75 ml/3 fl oz natural yogurt

salt and freshly ground
    black pepper
fresh thyme sprigs, to garnish

To serve:
natural yogurt
freshly cooked rice or noodles

Cut the chicken into finger-length strips and reserve. Heat a frying pan or wok, add half the oil and, when hot, add the chicken and cook over a high heat for 3–4 minutes until lightly browned, remove and reserve.

Wipe the pan clean, then heat the remaining oil and margarine or butter. Gently cook the onion for 5 minutes. Add the chestnut mushrooms and fry for a further 5 minutes, or until tender. Sprinkle in the thyme and cook for 30 seconds. Stir in the stock and return the chicken to the pan. Cook for 4–5 minutes until the chicken is cooked through and tender. Stir in the yogurt and heat until piping hot, do not allow to boil. Season to taste with salt and pepper. Garnish with sprigs of fresh thyme and serve immediately with a spoonful of yogurt and rice or noodles.

Spoon any remaining stroganoff onto a clean plate or dish and cover with clingfilm or lid. When cool, keep in the refrigerator for up to 2 days. You can freeze but may find that the sauce separates, if so, stir until blended. When wishing to reheat the stroganoff, cover with clean clingfilm and pierce 2–3 times. Heat on High in the microwave for 2 minutes then allow to stand for 1 minute. If not piping hot, return to the microwave and heat for a further minute. Stand for 1 minute then eat.

HELPFUL HINT.
Mushrooms should not be washed but wiped and their stalks trimmed.

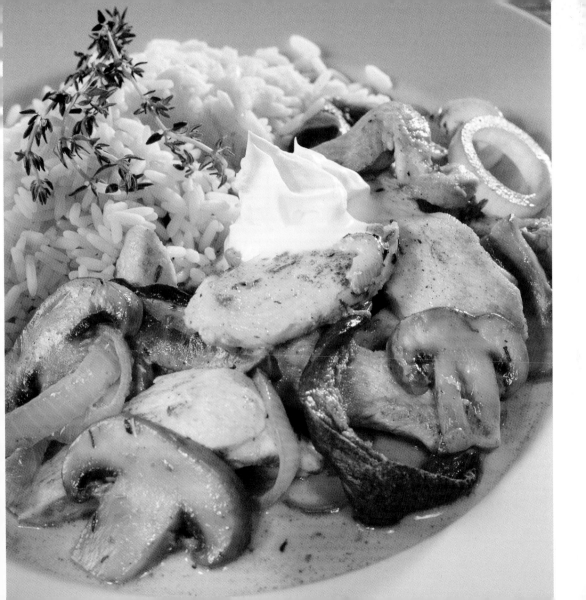

Tuna & Mushroom Ragout

MAKES 2 LARGE PORTIONS

125 g/4 oz basmati
and wild rice
25 g/1 oz margarine or butter
1 tbsp vegetable or olive oil
1 small onion, peeled and
finely chopped
1 garlic clove, peeled
and crushed

150 g/5 oz button
mushrooms, wiped
and halved
1 tbsp plain flour
200 g/7 oz canned tomatoes,
chopped
1 tsp freshly chopped parsley
dash of Worcestershire
sauce (optional)

200 g can tuna in oil, drained
salt and freshly ground
black pepper
2 tbsp Parmesan or
Cheddar cheese, grated
1 tsp freshly shredded basil

To serve:
green salad and garlic bread

Cook the basmati and wild rice in a saucepan of boiling salted water for 20 minutes, then drain and return to the pan. Stir in half of the margarine or butter, cover the pan and leave to stand for 2 minutes until all of the margarine or butter has melted.

Heat the oil and the remaining margarine or butter in a frying pan and cook the onion for 1–2 minutes until soft. Add the garlic and mushrooms and continue to cook for a further 3 minutes. Stir in the flour and cook for 1 minute, then add the canned tomatoes with their juice and bring the sauce to the boil. Add the parsley, Worcestershire sauce, if using, and tuna and simmer gently for 3 minutes. Season to taste with salt and freshly ground pepper.

TASTY TIP

Fresh basil adds a wonderful flavour and fragrance, but sometimes it can be difficult to find. Alternatively, use chopped tomatoes with basil already added to them, or use extra parsley.

Stir the rice well, place on two plates and spoon the tuna and mushroom mixture on top of the rice. Sprinkle with the grated cheese and the basil. Serve immediately with a green salad and chunks of garlic bread, if liked.

Any remaining ragout and rice can be placed on a clean plate, covered with clingfilm and left overnight in the refrigerator. Do not freeze. Next day, the ragout could be eaten cold as a salad. If you'd like it hot, cover with clean clingfilm, pierce 2–3 times, and heat on High in the microwave for 2 minutes. Allow to stand for 1 minute before eating.

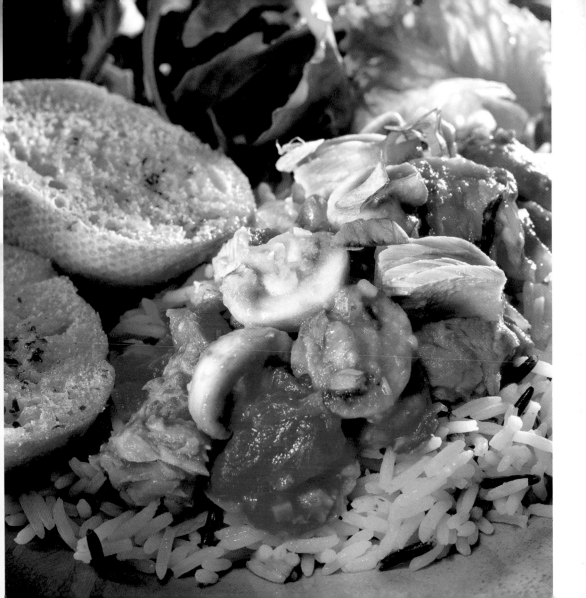

Egg & Bacon Pie

CUTS INTO 4–6 PORTIONS

225 g/8 oz bought
  shortcrust pastry
flour, for dusting

For the filling:
40 g/1½ oz margarine or butter

40 g/1½ oz plain white flour
450 ml/¾ pint milk, warmed
225 g/8 oz back bacon
  rashers, trimmed of fat
  and cut into small strips

salt and freshly ground
  black pepper
3 medium eggs, plus egg
  for brushing
chips and baked
  tomatoes, to serve

Preheat the oven to 200°C/400°F/Gas Mark 6, 15 minutes before required. Cut the pastry in half. Roll out on a lightly floured surface and use one half to line a deep 20.5 cm/8 inch pie dish. Melt the fat in a small pan and sprinkle in the flour. Cook over a medium heat for 2 minutes, stirring constantly, until thickened (it will form a slightly grainy paste). Draw off the heat and gradually stir in the warmed milk. Return to the heat, stirring constantly, until the mixture is thick enough to coat the back of a wooden spoon. Remove from the heat and add the bacon, a little at a time, and stir. Season to taste and leave to cool.

Beat the eggs and then stir them into the cooled sauce. Spoon the mixture into the pastry-lined dish. Roll the remaining pastry out to form a lid for the top of the pie. Lightly brush the pastry on the edge of the dish with egg or cold water. Wrap the pastry lid around the rolling pin and place in position over the pie dish. Press the edges together firmly and trim. Make a decorative edge round the pie. Brush the top of the pie with beaten egg and cut slits across the top to allow the steam to escape. Place on a baking sheet and bake in the preheated oven. After 15 minutes, reduce the oven temperature to 180°C/350°F/Gas Mark 4. Brush the top of the pie again with the beaten egg. Continue to bake for a further 20–25 minutes until the pie is golden and the filling has set. Serve warm or cold with chips and baked tomatoes.

This pie will keep for 3–4 days in the refrigerator. It is good eaten cold. Once cool, cover the top with clingfilm and keep in the refrigerator. I would not recommend freezing or reheating.

Shepherd's Pie

MAKES 3 LARGE PORTIONS

1 tbsp vegetable or olive oil
1 onion, peeled and
   finely chopped
1 carrot, peeled and
   finely chopped
1 celery stalk, trimmed and
   finely chopped

450 g/1 lb fresh lean lamb mince
1 tbsp plain flour
2–3 sprigs of fresh thyme
150–200 ml/5–7 fl oz lamb or
   vegetable stock
2 tbsp tomato purée
salt and freshly ground

black pepper
575 g/1¼ lb potatoes, peeled
   and cut into chunks
1 tbsp margarine or butter
3–4 tbsp milk
1 tbsp freshly chopped parsley
fresh herbs, to garnish (optional)

TASTY TIP

A traditional shepherd's pie is always made from cold roast lamb, but you'll probably find it easier to use fresh minced lamb as instructed.

Preheat the oven to 200°C/400°F/Gas Mark 6, about 15 minutes before cooking. Heat the oil in a large saucepan and add the onion, carrot and celery. Cook over a medium heat for 5 minutes, add the lamb and fry for a further 5 minutes, stirring frequently until the lamb has browned. Add the flour and cook for 2 minutes before adding the thyme, then stir in 150 ml/5 fl oz of the stock and the tomato purée. Season to taste with salt and pepper and simmer gently for 10 minutes until reduced and thickened, adding a little more stock if necessary (you want a moist, not wet, consistency). Remove from the heat to cool slightly and adjust seasoning if required.

Meanwhile, boil the potatoes in plenty of salted water for 12–15 minutes until tender. Drain and return to the saucepan over a low heat to dry out. Remove from the heat and add the margarine or butter, milk and parsley. Mash until creamy, adding a little more milk if necessary. Season. Transfer the lamb mixture to an ovenproof dish, spoon over the mash and spread evenly to cover completely. Fork the surface, place on a baking sheet, then cook in the oven for 25–30 minutes until the topping is browned and the filling is piping hot. Garnish and serve.

Spoon any remaining pie onto plates or into containers. Once cool, cover with clingfilm or a lid. Keep for up to 2 days in the refrigerator, or label and date then freeze for up to 2 weeks. Thaw in the refrigerator overnight. To reheat, spoon a portion onto a plate, cover with clingfilm and pierce 2–3 times. Heat in the microwave on High for 2 minutes 20 seconds. Allow to stand for 1 minute, then, if not piping hot, reheat for a further minute.

Traditional Fish Pie

MAKES 3 LARGE PORTIONS

350 g/12 oz fresh haddock
  or coley fillets, skinned
450 ml/¾ pint milk
1 small onion, peeled and
  quartered
salt and freshly ground
  black pepper

450 g/1 lb potatoes, peeled
  and cut into chunks
40 g/1½ oz margarine
  or butter
50 g/2 oz large prawns or
  thawed peeled prawns
  (optional)

2 medium eggs, hard-boiled
  and quartered
125 g/4 oz canned or thawed
  frozen sweetcorn, drained
2 tsp freshly chopped parsley
3 tbsp plain flour
2 tbsp Cheddar cheese, grated

Preheat the oven to 200°C/400°F/Gas Mark 6, about 15 minutes before cooking. Place the fish in a shallow frying pan, pour over 300 ml/½ pint of the milk and add the onion. Season to taste with salt and pepper. Bring to the boil and simmer for 8–10 minutes until the fish is cooked (carefully check and remove any bones from the cooked fish). Remove the fish with a slotted spoon and place in a 900ml/1½ pint baking dish. Strain the cooking liquid and reserve. Boil the potatoes until soft, then mash with half the margarine or butter and 1–2 tablespoons of the remaining milk. Reserve. Arrange the prawns, if using, and sliced eggs on top of the fish, then scatter over the sweetcorn and sprinkle with the parsley.

Melt the remaining margarine or butter in a saucepan, stir in the flour and cook gently for 1 minute, stirring. Whisk in the reserved cooking liquid and remaining milk. Cook for 2 minutes, or until thickened, then pour over the fish and cool slightly. Spread the mashed potato over the top and sprinkle over the cheese. Bake in the oven for 30 minutes until golden. Serve immediately.

TASTY TIP

Any variety of white fish may be used in this delicious dish such as hake, ling, pollack and whiting. You could also used smoked fish, such as smoked cod or haddock for a change.

Keep any remaining cooled cooked fish pie on a couple of plates covered with clingfilm overnight in the refrigerator. Or, freeze in a container with a lid. Label and date. Keep for up to 2 weeks and thaw in the refrigerator overnight. To reheat, spoon portions onto plates, cover with clingfilm and pierce 2–3 times. Heat in the microwave on High for 2 minutes 20 seconds. Allow to stand for 1 minute, then, if not piping hot, reheat for an extra minute.

Beef Cooked in Beer

MAKES 2 PORTIONS

275 g/10 oz stewing or
  braising steak
2 tbsp margarine or butter
1 large onion, peeled and
  thinly sliced
1–2 garlic cloves, peeled
  and thinly sliced

15 g/½ oz plain flour
1 tsp mustard powder
150 ml/¼ pint beef stock
300 ml/½ pint beer (light ale)
1–2 tsp sugar
2 fresh bay leaves
freshly ground black pepper

1 tsp freshly chopped
  parsley, to garnish
mashed potatoes and
  freshly cooked seasonal
  green vegetables,
  to serve

Preheat the oven to 160°C/325°F/Gas Mark 3, 10 minutes before required. Trim the beef, discarding any sinew, gristle or fat. Cut into strips about 5 cm/2 inches long. Melt the margarine or butter in a heavy-based saucepan over a low heat and add the onions and garlic. Cook, stirring frequently, for 12 minutes, or until the onion has softened and started to brown. Remove with a slotted spoon, place on a plate and reserve.

Add the beef to the margarine or butter remaining in the saucepan and cook, stirring frequently, for 5–8 minutes until the meat is sealed. Return the onion and garlic to the pan and stir lightly. Sprinkle in the flour and mustard powder and cook, stirring, for 2 minutes. Turn the heat off underneath the pan and gradually stir in the stock and then the beer. Return to the heat and bring to the boil, stirring. Sprinkle over the sugar and add the bay leaves and black pepper to taste, then transfer to a casserole dish. Cover with the lid, place in the preheated oven and cook for 2–2½ hours until the meat is tender. Remove the bay leaves, adjust the seasoning, then sprinkle with parsley and serve with freshly cooked vegetables.

Once cool, refrigerate any remaining stew on a plate covered with clingfilm or in a container with a lid for up to 3 days. Or, freeze in a freezer bag, labelled and dated, for up to 1 month. Thaw overnight in the refrigerator. Reheat in a clean dish covered with clingfilm and pierced 2–3 times in the microwave on High for 2 minutes. Allow to stand for 1 minute. If not piping hot, reheat for a further minute. Or, reheat on the hob for 8–10 minutes, stirring occasionally until piping hot.

Cassoulet

MAKES 2 PORTIONS

1 tbsp vegetable or olive oil
1 onion, peeled and chopped
1 celery stalk, trimmed and
    chopped
2 carrots, peeled and sliced
2–3 garlic cloves, peeled
    and crushed

225 g/8 oz pork belly (optional)
4 spicy thick sausages
few fresh thyme sprigs
salt and freshly ground
    black pepper
400 g can cannellini beans,
    drained and rinsed

600 ml/1 pint
    vegetable stock
50 g/2 oz fresh breadcrumbs
2 tbsp freshly
    chopped thyme

Preheat the oven to 180°C/350°F/Gas Mark 4. Heat the oil in a large saucepan or flameproof casserole, add the onion, celery, carrots and garlic and fry for 5 minutes. Cut the pork, if using, into small pieces and cut the sausages into chunks. Add the meat to the vegetables and cook, stirring, until lightly browned. Add the thyme sprigs and season to taste with salt and pepper. If a saucepan was used, transfer everything to an ovenproof casserole. Spoon the beans on top, then pour in the stock. Mix the breadcrumbs with 1 tablespoon of the chopped thyme in a small bowl and sprinkle on top of the beans. Cover with a lid and cook in the oven for 40 minutes. Remove the lid and cook for a further 15 minutes, or until the breadcrumbs are crisp. Sprinkle with the remaining chopped thyme and serve.

Any remaining cassoulet can be frozen. When cool, spoon into a container and cover with a lid. Label and date then freeze. Use within 2 weeks and thaw overnight in the refrigerator when required. Or, keep for up to 2–3 days in the refrigerator. Spoon the cassoulet into a dish and cover with clingfilm. To reheat, spoon into a clean dish and cover with clingfilm. Pierce 2–3 times. Heat on High for 2 minutes in the microwave, allow to stand for 1 minute and, if not piping hot, reheat for 1 minute, stand for a further minute, then eat. Alternatively, reheat on the hob. Spoon into a saucepan and heat gently. Bring to the boil, reduce to a simmer and heat for 8–10 minutes. Stir occasionally and, when piping hot, stir and eat.

TASTY TIP

Replace the pork belly
with lardons, if you prefer.

Tuna Fish Burgers

MAKES 2 PORTIONS

350 g/12 oz potatoes, peeled
   and cut into chunks
1 tbsp margarine or butter
1–2 tbsp milk
350 g/12 oz canned tuna in oil
2 spring onions, trimmed
   and finely chopped

1 tbsp freshly chopped parsley
salt and freshly ground
   black pepper
2 small eggs, beaten
2 tbsp seasoned plain flour
50 g/2 oz fresh white
   breadcrumbs

2 tbsp veg. or sunflower oil
4 sesame seed baps (optional)

To serve:
fat chips
mixed salad
tomato chutney

Place the potatoes in a large saucepan, cover with boiling water and simmer for 12–15 minutes until soft. Drain, then mash with the margarine or butter and sufficient milk to give a stiff mixture. (To ensure the mixture isn't too soft to shape, after draining the potatoes thoroughly, dry them over a very low heat before mashing with the milk and butter.) Turn into a large bowl. Drain the tuna, discarding the oil and flake into the bowl of potato. Stir well to mix. Add the spring onions and parsley to the mixture and season to taste with salt and pepper. Add 1 tablespoon of the beaten egg to bind the mixture together. Chill in the refrigerator for at least 1 hour. Shape the chilled mixture with your hands into 4 large burgers. First, coat the burgers with seasoned flour, then brush them with the remaining beaten egg, allowing any excess to drip back into the bowl. Finally, coat them evenly in the breadcrumbs, pressing the crumbs on with your hands, if necessary. If time allows, cover the bread-coated burgers with clingfilm and chill in the refrigerator for 30 minutes before cooking so that they are really firm.

Heat a little of the oil in a frying pan and fry the burgers for 2–3 minutes on each side until golden, adding more oil if necessary. Drain on absorbent kitchen paper and serve hot in baps, if using, with chips, mixed salad and chutney.

The burgers can be refrigerated for up to 2 days covered lightly with clingfilm or frozen for 2 weeks. Thaw overnight in the refrigerator. When ready to eat, heat a little vegetable oil in a frying pan and fry on both sides for 3 minutes to crisp and heat through. Drain on kitchen paper.

Chicken Pie with Sweet Potato Topping

MAKES 4 LARGE PORTIONS

575g/1¼ lb sweet potatoes, peeled and cut into chunks
salt and freshly ground black pepper
4–5 tbsp milk
25 g/1 oz margarine or butter
2 tsp brown sugar

grated zest of 1 orange
450 g/1 lb boneless, skinless chicken meat such as breast
1 medium onion, peeled and coarsely chopped
125 g/4 oz button mushrooms, stems trimmed

1 large leek, trimmed and thickly sliced
150 ml/¼ pint water
1 chicken stock cube
1 tbsp freshly chopped parsley
50 ml/2 fl oz natural yogurt
green vegetables, to serve

Preheat the oven to 190°C/375°F/Gas Mark 5, 10 minutes before required. Cook the potatoes in lightly salted boiling water until tender. Drain well, then return to the saucepan and mash until smooth and creamy, gradually adding the milk, then the margarine or butter, sugar and orange zest. Season to taste with salt and pepper and reserve.

Place the chicken in a saucepan with the onion, mushrooms, leek, water and stock cube and season to taste. Simmer, covered for 20 minutes, until the vegetables are tender. Using a slotted spoon, transfer the chicken and vegetables to a 1.1 litre/2 pint pie dish. Add the parsley and yogurt to the liquid in the pan and bring to the boil. Simmer until thickened and smooth, stirring constantly. Pour over the chicken in the pie dish, mix and cool.

Spread the mashed sweet potato over the chicken filling, and swirl the surface into decorative peaks. Bake in the preheated oven for 35 minutes, or until the top is golden and the chicken filling is piping hot. Serve immediately with fresh green vegetables.

Keep any remaining pie in lidded containers or on a plate covered with clingfilm in the refrigerator for up to 2 days or freeze for up to 2 weeks. If freezing, label and date and thaw overnight in the refrigerator. Reheat in a clean dish, covered with clingfilm and pierced 2–3 times, in the microwave on High for 2 minutes 30 seconds. Stand for 1 minute. If not piping hot, heat for an extra minute.

Impress
Your Friends

Classic Minestrone

MAKES 6–8 PORTIONS

25 g/1 oz butter
  or margarine
3 tbsp vegetable or olive oil
3 rashers streaky bacon
1 large onion, peeled
1 garlic clove, peeled
1 celery stalk, trimmed
2 carrots, peeled

400 g can tomatoes,
  chopped
1.1 litre/2 pints chicken stock
125 g/4 oz green cabbage,
  finely shredded
50 g/2 oz French beans,
  trimmed and halved
3 tbsp frozen peas

50 g/2 oz spaghetti, broken
  into short pieces
salt and freshly ground
  black pepper
Parmesan cheese shavings,
  to garnish
crusty bread, to serve

Heat the butter or margarine and oil together in a large saucepan. Chop the bacon and add to the saucepan. Cook for 3–4 minutes, and then remove with a slotted spoon and reserve.

Finely chop the onion, garlic, celery and carrots and add to the saucepan, one ingredient at a time, stirring well after each addition. Cover and cook gently for 8–10 minutes until the vegetables are softened. Add the chopped tomatoes, with their juice and the stock, bring to the boil then cover the saucepan with a lid, reduce the heat and simmer gently for about 20 minutes. Stir in the cabbage, beans, peas and spaghetti pieces. Cover and simmer for a further 20 minutes, or until all the ingredients are tender. Season to taste with salt and pepper.

Return the cooked bacon to the saucepan and bring the soup to the boil. Serve the soup immediately with Parmesan cheese shavings sprinkled on the top and plenty of crusty bread to accompany it.

Any remaining minestrone will not freeze, but will keep well overnight in the refrigerator. Pour into a clean bowl and, when cool, cover with clingfilm and refrigerate. When ready to reheat, pour into a saucepan and place over a gentle heat. Heat for 8–10 minutes until piping hot.

TASTY TIP

There are many different variations of minestrone. You can add drained canned cannellini beans either in place of or as well as the spaghetti, or use small soup pasta shells.

Creamy Turkey & Tomato Pasta

MAKES 4 PORTIONS

3 tbsp vegetable or olive oil
350 g/12 oz turkey breasts,
    cut into bite-sized pieces
275 g/10 oz cherry tomatoes
2 garlic cloves, peeled
    and chopped

3 tbsp vinegar, such as malt
    or balsamic
salt and freshly ground
    black pepper
350 g/12 oz tagliatelle
2 tbsp freshly chopped basil

200 ml tub crème fraîche or
    natural yogurt
shaved Parmesan or mature
    Cheddar cheese,
    to garnish

Preheat the oven to 200°C/400°F/Gas Mark 6. Heat 2 tablespoons of the oil in a large frying pan. Add the turkey and cook for 5 minutes, or until sealed, turning occasionally. Transfer to a roasting tin and add the remaining oil, the tomatoes, garlic and vinegar. Stir well and season to taste with salt and pepper. Roast for 30 minutes, or until the turkey is tender, turning the food once.

Meanwhile, bring a large pan of lightly salted water to a rolling boil. Add the pasta and cook according to the packet instructions, or until *al dente*. Drain, return to the pan and keep warm.

Stir the basil and seasoning into the crème fraîche or yogurt. Remove the tin from the oven. Stir the crème fraîche or yogurt mix into the turkey and tomatoes and return to the oven for 1–2 minutes, until piping hot. Stir the mixture into the pasta and toss lightly together. Tip into a warmed serving dish. Garnish with Parmesan cheese shavings and serve immediately.

This dish does not freeze well, but will keep in the refrigerator overnight. Once cool, spoon into a clean bowl, cover with clingfilm and place in the refrigerator. To reheat, make 2–3 slits in the clingfilm and heat on High in the microwave for 2 minutes. Remove and allow to stand for 1 minute. Stir, adding a little extra yogurt or water if there is very little sauce. If the pasta and turkey are not piping hot, return to the microwave for a further minute. The pasta can also be reheated in a saucepan on the hob. Spoon into a clean saucepan, preferably nonstick, with 1–2 tablespoons water. Heat over a medium heat, stirring frequently for 8–10 minutes until piping hot.

Leek & Ham Risotto

MAKES 4 PORTIONS

1 tbsp vegetable or olive oil
25 g/1 oz butter or
　margarine
1 medium onion, peeled
　and finely chopped
4 leeks, trimmed and
　thinly sliced

1½ tbsp freshly chopped
　thyme or use 1 tsp
　dried thyme
350 g/12 oz arborio rice
1.25 litres/2¼ pints vegetable
　or chicken stock, heated
225 g/8 oz cooked ham

175 g/6 oz peas,
　thawed if frozen
50 g/2 oz Parmesan or
　Cheddar cheese, grated
salt and freshly ground
　black pepper

Heat the oil and half the butter or margarine together in a large saucepan. Add the onion and leeks and cook over a medium heat for 6–8 minutes, stirring occasionally, until soft and beginning to colour. Stir in the thyme and cook briefly. Add the rice and stir well. Continue stirring over a medium heat for about 1 minute until the rice is glossy. Add a ladleful or two of the stock and stir well until the stock is absorbed. Continue adding stock, a ladleful at a time, and stirring well between additions, until about two-thirds of the stock has been added.

Meanwhile, either chop or finely shred the ham, then add to the saucepan of rice together with the peas. Continue adding ladlefuls of stock, as described above, until the rice is creamy and tender but with just a slight bite to it and the ham is heated thoroughly. You do not have to add all of the liquid. Add the remaining butter or margarine, sprinkle over the cheese and season to taste with salt and pepper. When the butter or margarine has melted and the cheese has softened, stir well to incorporate. Taste and adjust the seasoning, then serve immediately.

Rice does not freeze well and incorrect handling can result in food poisoning. However, any remaining risotto will keep overnight in the refrigerator, spooned into a dish and covered with clingfilm. To reheat, pierce the clingfilm in 2–3 places and heat on High for 2 minutes. Allow to stand for 1 minute then stir. If not piping hot, heat for a further minute. Or, heat the risotto gently in a pan with a little extra oil, stirring, until piping hot. If becoming dry, add a little stock.

Chicken & White Wine Risotto

MAKES 4 PORTIONS

2 tbsp olive or vegetable oil
125 g/4 oz unsalted butter
or margarine
2 shallots, peeled and
finely chopped
275 g/10 oz arborio rice

600 ml/1 pint white wine or
extra chicken stock
750 ml/1¼ pints chicken
stock, heated
275 g/10 oz skinless chicken
breast fillets, thinly sliced

50 g/2 oz Parmesan or
Cheddar cheese, grated
2 tbsp freshly chopped
dill or parsley
salt and freshly ground
black pepper

HELPFUL HINT
Keeping the stock at a low
simmer in a separate
saucepan will ensure that the
dish is kept at a constant
heat during cooking, which is
important to achieve a
perfect creamy texture.

Heat the oil and half the butter or margarine in a large heavy-based saucepan or frying pan over a medium-high heat. Add the shallots and cook for 2 minutes, or until softened, stirring frequently. Add the rice and cook for 2–3 minutes, stirring frequently, until the rice is translucent and well coated. Pour in half the wine, if using, it will bubble and steam rapidly; otherwise use 300 ml/½ pint stock. Cook, stirring constantly, until the liquid is absorbed. Add a ladleful of the hot stock and cook until the liquid is absorbed. Carefully stir in the chicken.

Continue adding the stock, about half a ladleful at a time, allowing each addition to be absorbed before adding the next; never allow the rice to cook dry. This process should take about 20 minutes. The risotto should have a creamy consistency and the rice should be tender, but firm to the bite. Stir in the remaining wine or 300 ml/½ pint stock and cook for 2–3 minutes. Remove from the heat and stir in the remaining butter or margarine with the cheese and half the chopped herbs. Season to taste with salt and pepper. Spoon into warmed shallow bowls and sprinkle each with the remaining chopped herbs. Serve immediately.

Any remaining risotto will keep overnight in the refrigerator, spooned into a dish and covered with clingfilm. To reheat, pierce the clingfilm in 2–3 places and heat on High for 2 minutes. Allow to stand for 1 minute then stir. If not piping hot, heat for a further minute. Or, heat the risotto gently in a pan with a little extra oil, stirring, until piping hot. If becoming dry, add a little stock.

Slow Roast Chicken with Potatoes & Oregano

MAKES 6 PORTIONS

1.4–1.8 kg/3–4 lb
  oven-ready chicken
1 lemon, halved
1 onion, peeled and
  quartered
50 g/2 oz butter or

margarine, softened
salt and freshly ground
  black pepper
1 kg/2¼ lb potatoes, peeled
  and quartered
3–4 tbsp vegetable or olive oil

1 tbsp dried oregano,
  crumbled
1 tsp fresh thyme leaves
2 tbsp freshly chopped thyme
fresh sage leaves,
  to garnish

Preheat the oven to 200°C/400°F/Gas Mark 6. Rinse the chicken and dry well, inside and out, with absorbent kitchen paper. Rub the chicken all over with the lemon halves, and then squeeze the juice over it and into the cavity. Put the squeezed halves into the cavity with the quartered onion. Rub the softened butter or margarine all over the chicken and season to taste with salt and pepper, and then put it in a large roasting tin, breast-side down.

Toss the potatoes in the oil, season with salt and pepper to taste and add the dried oregano and fresh thyme. Arrange the potatoes with the oil around the chicken and carefully pour 150 ml/¼ pint water into one end of the pan (not over the oil). Roast in the oven for 25 minutes. Reduce the temperature to 190°C/375°F/Gas Mark 5 and turn the chicken breast-side up. Turn the potatoes, sprinkle over half the fresh herbs and baste the chicken and potatoes with the juices. Continue roasting for 1 hour, or until the chicken is cooked, basting occasionally. If the liquid evaporates completely, add a little more water. The chicken is done when the juices run clear when the thigh is pierced with a skewer. Transfer the chicken to a carving board and rest for 5 minutes, covered with kitchen foil. Return the potatoes to the oven while the chicken is resting. Carve the chicken into serving pieces and arrange on a large serving dish. Arrange the potatoes around the chicken and drizzle over any remaining juices. Sprinkle with the remaining herbs and serve.

Any remaining chicken meat can be placed on a plate, covered with clingfilm or kitchen foil and left in the refrigerator for up to 2 days. Use in risottos, pasta sauces or as a filling for omelettes. If reheating, ensure that the chicken is piping hot before eating.

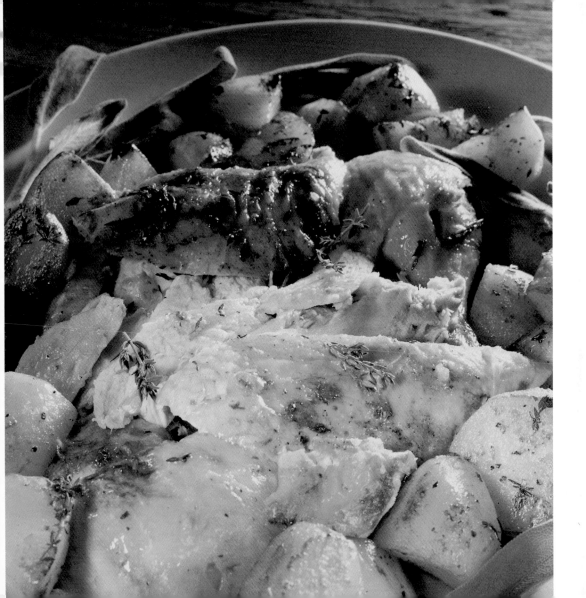

Lemon Chicken with Potatoes, Rosemary & Olives

MAKES 6 PORTIONS

12 skinless boneless
  chicken thighs
1 large lemon
125 ml/4 fl oz vegetable
  or olive oil
4–6 garlic cloves, peeled
  and sliced

2 onions, peeled and
  thinly sliced
4–6 fresh rosemary sprigs
1.1 kg/2½ lb potatoes,
  peeled and cut into
  4 cm/1½ inch pieces

salt and freshly ground
  black pepper
18–24 black olives,
  pitted (optional)
freshly cooked carrots
  and courgettes, to serve

Preheat oven to 200°C/400°F/Gas Mark 6, 15 minutes before cooking. Trim the chicken thighs and place in a shallow baking dish large enough to hold them in a single layer. Remove the zest from the lemon and cut into thin strips. Reserve half and add the remainder to the chicken. Squeeze the lemon juice over the chicken, toss to coat well and leave to stand for 10 minutes.

Add the remaining lemon strips, oil, garlic, onions and half of the rosemary sprigs. Toss gently and leave for about 20 minutes.

Cover the potatoes with lightly salted water and bring to the boil. Cook for 2 minutes, then drain well and add to the chicken. Season to taste with salt and pepper.

HELPFUL HINT

It is worth seeking out unwaxed lemons for any recipe in which the zest is to be eaten. If unwaxed are unavailable, pour hot water over them and scrub well before removing the zest.

Roast the chicken in the preheated oven for 50 minutes, turning frequently and basting, or until the chicken is cooked. Just before the end of cooking time, discard the rosemary, and add fresh sprigs of rosemary. Add the olives, if using, and stir. Serve immediately with the carrots and courgettes.

Any remaining chicken thighs can be cooled, placed on a clean plate and covered with kitchen foil. Keep in the refrigerator for up to 2 days. Do not reheat the chicken thighs on their own as they will be dry. Use when making pasta or rice dishes, as part of a topping for pizza or cold with salad.

Chicken & Summer Vegetable Risotto

MAKES 4 PORTIONS

1 litre/1¾ pint chicken
 or vegetable stock
125 g/4 oz baby asparagus
 spears (optional)
175 g/6 oz French beans
15 g/½ oz butter
 or margarine

1 small onion, peeled
 and finely chopped
275 g/10 oz arborio rice
½ tsp turmeric
75 g/3 oz frozen peas,
 thawed

225 g/8 oz cooked chicken,
 skinned and diced
juice of ½ lemon
salt and freshly ground
 black pepper
25 g/1 oz Parmesan or
 Cheddar cheese, shaved

Bring the stock to the boil in a large saucepan. Trim the asparagus, if using, and cut into 4 cm/1½ inch lengths. Blanch the asparagus in the stock for 1–2 minutes until tender, and then remove with a slotted spoon and reserve. Halve the green beans and cook in the boiling stock for 4 minutes. Remove and reserve. Turn down the heat and keep the stock barely simmering.

Melt the butter or margarine in a heavy-based saucepan. Add the onion and cook gently for about 5 minutes. Add the rice and cook, stirring for 1 minute until the grains are coated and look translucent. Add the turmeric and a ladle of the stock. Simmer, stirring all the time, until the stock has absorbed. Continue adding the stock, a ladle at a time, waiting for it to absorb. After 15 minutes the risotto should be creamy with a slight bite to it. If not, add a little more stock and cook for a few more minutes, or until ready. Add the peas, reserved vegetables, chicken and lemon juice. Season to taste with salt and pepper and cook for 3–4 minutes until the chicken is thoroughly heated and piping hot. Spoon the risotto on to warmed serving plates. Scatter each portion with a few shavings of Parmesan or Cheddar cheese and serve immediately.

Any remaining risotto will keep overnight in the refrigerator, spooned into a dish and covered with clingfilm. To reheat, pierce the clingfilm in 2–3 places and heat on High for 2 minutes. Allow to stand for 1 minute then stir. If not piping hot, heat for a further minute. Or, heat the risotto gently in a pan with a little extra oil, stirring, until piping hot. If becoming dry, add a little stock.

Pork Chop Hotpot

MAKES 4 PORTIONS

4 pork chops
flour for dusting
225 g/8 oz shallots, peeled
2 garlic cloves, peeled
50 g/2 oz sun-dried tomatoes
    or 2 ripe fresh tomatoes
2 tbsp vegetable or olive oil

400 g can plum tomatoes
300 ml/½ pint chicken stock
2 tbsp tomato purée
2 tbsp freshly chopped
    oregano, or 2 tsp dried
salt and freshly ground
    black pepper

fresh oregano leaves,
    to garnish (optional)

To serve:
freshly cooked new potatoes
French beans

TASTY TIP

Other meat can be
used if liked. Try lamb
chops, chicken portions
or sausages.

Preheat oven to 190°C/375°F/Gas Mark 5, 10 minutes before cooking. Trim the pork chops, removing any excess fat, wipe with a clean, damp cloth, then dust with a little flour and reserve. Cut the shallots in half if large. Chop the garlic and chop the sun-dried or fresh tomatoes. Heat the oil in a large flameproof casserole dish and cook the pork for about 5 minutes, turning occasionally, until browned all over. Using a slotted spoon, lift out of the dish and reserve. Add the shallots and cook for 5 minutes, stirring occasionally. Return the pork to the dish and scatter with the garlic and sun-dried or fresh tomatoes, and then pour over the can of tomatoes with their juice.

Blend the stock and tomato purée together and add the oregano. Season to taste with salt and pepper, then pour over the pork and bring to a gentle boil. Cover with a close-fitting lid and cook in the oven for 1 hour, or until the pork is tender. Adjust the seasoning to taste, scatter with a few oregano leaves, if using, and serve immediately with freshly cooked potatoes and beans.

Any remaining pork chops and sauce can be placed in a dish. Either label and date and freeze for up to 1 month or cover and refrigerate for up to 2 days. If frozen, allow to thaw overnight in the refrigerator before using. To reheat, place in the casserole dish in the oven at 180°C/350°F/Gas Mark 4 for 20 minutes, or until piping hot. Add a little extra stock if becoming too dry. Or, place in a heavy-based saucepan on the hob and bring to the boil. Reduce to a gentle simmer for 20 minutes, or until piping hot. Add a little extra stock if necessary.

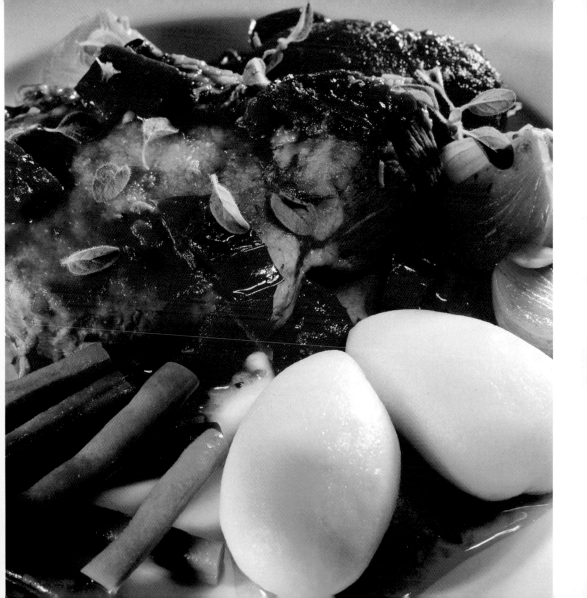

Toad in the Hole

MAKES 4 PORTIONS

8 large pork sausages
125 g/4 oz plain flour
pinch salt
2 medium eggs

225 ml/8 fl oz milk
1 tbsp sunflower or
   vegetable oil

To serve:
seasonal vegetables
English mustard

Preheat the oven to 220˚C/425˚F/Gas Mark 7, 15 minutes before required. Lightly prick the sausages and reserve.

Sieve the flour and salt into a mixing bowl and make a well in the centre. Drop the eggs into the well and then, using a wooden spoon, beat in the eggs, drawing the flour in from the sides of the bowl. Gradually add the milk and beat to form a smooth batter without any lumps. Allow to stand for 30 minutes.

When ready to cook, pour the oil into a 25.5 x 20.5 cm/10 x 8 inch roasting tin. Heat until almost smoking and then add the sausages. Carefully turn the sausages in the hot oil and return to the oven for 5 minutes.

Remove from the oven and turn them over again. Stir the batter well and pour over the sausages. Return to the oven and cook for 35–40 minutes until the pudding is well risen and golden brown. Serve immediately with seasonal vegetables and English mustard.

Toad in the hole does not freeze or keep well overnight in the refrigerator. You simply have to eat it all, so get your friends round!

Treats & Desserts

Chocolate Chip Cookies

MAKES 18

75 g/3 oz plain flour
pinch of salt
½ tsp baking powder
40 g/1½ oz butter
　or margarine

50 g/2 oz soft light
　brown sugar
1½ tbsp golden syrup
50 g/2 oz chocolate chips

Preheat the oven to 190°C/375°F/Gas Mark 5, 10 minutes before baking. Lightly oil 1–2 large baking sheets.

In a large bowl, sift together the flour, salt and baking powder.

Cut the butter or margarine into small pieces and add to the flour mixture. Using 2 knives or the fingertips, rub in the butter or margarine until the mixture resembles coarse breadcrumbs. Add the light brown sugar, golden syrup and chocolate chips. Mix together until a smooth dough forms.

Shape the mixture into small balls and arrange on the baking sheet, leaving enough space to allow them to expand. (These cookies do not increase in size by a great deal, but allow a little space for expansion.) Flatten the mixture slightly with the fingertips or the heel of the hand.

TASTY TIP

This is a good basic cookie recipe to which many ingredients, like nuts, glacé cherries, chopped angelica, banana chips, dried cranberries or raisins, can be added instead of chocolate chips.

Bake in the preheated oven for 12–15 minutes until golden and cooked through. Allow to cool slightly, and then transfer the biscuits onto a wire rack to cool. Serve when cold or otherwise store in an airtight tin.

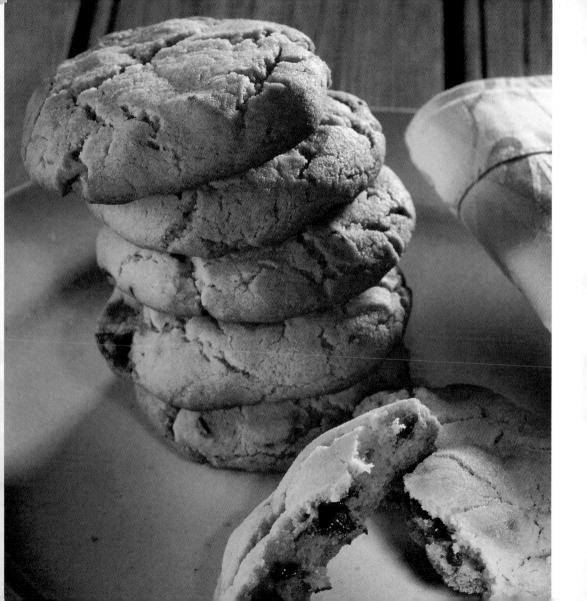

Chocolate Fudge Brownies

MAKES 16

125 g/4 oz butter
  or margarine
175 g/6 oz dark chocolate,
  roughly chopped
  or broken

225 g/8 oz caster sugar
2 tsp vanilla extract
2 medium eggs,
  lightly beaten
150 g/5 oz plain flour

For the icing:
175 g/6 oz icing sugar
2 tbsp cocoa powder
15 g/½ oz butter or
  margarine

Preheat the oven to 180°C/350°F/Gas Mark 4, 10 minutes before baking. Lightly oil and line a 20.5 cm/8 inch square cake tin with greaseproof or baking paper.

Slowly melt the butter or margarine and chocolate together in a heatproof bowl placed over a saucepan of simmering water. Transfer the mixture to a large bowl.

Stir in the sugar and vanilla extract, and then stir in the eggs. Sift over the flour and fold together well with a metal spoon or rubber spatula. Pour into the prepared tin.

Transfer to the preheated oven and bake for 30 minutes until just set. Remove the cooked mixture from the oven and leave to cool in the tin before turning it out on to a wire rack.

Sift the icing sugar and cocoa powder into a small bowl and make a well in the centre.

HELPFUL HINT

Do not place cake and biscuits in the same tin – the biscuits will go soggy. Plastic containers are not as good as metal, as they can make the baked goods taste 'musty'.

Place the butter or margarine in the well then gradually add 1–2 tablespoons of hot water (when making icing, add the liquid a little at a time; this way you will be able to get the correct consistency). Mix to form a smooth spreadable icing.

Pour the icing over the cooked mixture. Allow the icing to set before cutting into squares. Serve the brownies when they are cold. Keep in an airtight tin for up to 1 week.

Classic Flapjacks

MAKES 12

175 g/6 oz butter or
   margarine, plus extra
   for greasing
125 g/4 oz demerara sugar

2 tbsp golden syrup
175 g/6 oz jumbo
porridge oats
few drops vanilla extract

Preheat the oven to 160°C/325°F/Gas Mark 3. Butter a 20.5 cm/8 inch square baking tin.

Place the butter or margarine, sugar and golden syrup in a saucepan and heat gently until the butter has melted and every grain of sugar has dissolved.

Remove from the heat and stir in the oats and vanilla extract. Stir well and then spoon the mixture into the prepared tin.

Smooth level with the back of a large spoon. Bake in the centre of the oven for 30–40 minutes until golden. Leave to cool in the tin for 10 minutes, then mark into fingers and leave in the tin until completely cold. When cold, cut into fingers with a sharp knife.

Store in an airtight tin for up to 1 week.

TASTY TIP

If liked, add some dried fruit or nuts to the basic flapjack recipes. Try 50 g/2 oz raisins or cranberries or 50 g/2 oz chopped hazel nuts or flaked almonds.

Lemon Drizzle Cake

CUTS INTO 9

125 g/4 oz butter
  or margarine
175 g/6 oz caster sugar
2 large eggs

175 g/6 oz self-raising flour
2 lemons, preferably
  unwaxed
50 g/2 oz granulated sugar

Preheat the oven to 180°C/350°F/Gas Mark 4, 10 minutes before baking. Lightly oil and line the base of an 18 cm/7 inch square cake tin with baking paper. In a large bowl, cream the butter or margarine and sugar together until soft and fluffy.

Beat the eggs, then gradually add a little of the egg to the creamed mixture, adding 1 tablespoon of flour after each addition.

Finely grate the zest from 1 of the lemons and stir into the creamed mixture, beating well until smooth. Squeeze the juice from the lemon, strain, and then stir into the mixture. Spoon into the prepared tin, level the surface and bake in the preheated oven for 25–30 minutes. Using a zester, remove the peel from the last lemon and mix with 25 g/1 oz of the granulated sugar and reserve.

Squeeze the juice into a small saucepan. Add the rest of the granulated sugar to the lemon juice in the saucepan and heat gently, stirring occasionally. When the sugar has dissolved, simmer gently for 3–4 minutes until syrupy.

With a cocktail stick or fine skewer prick the cake all over. Sprinkle the lemon zest and sugar syrup over the top of the cake, drizzle over the syrup and leave to cool in the tin. Cut the cake into squares and serve.

Store for 1 week in an airtight tin.

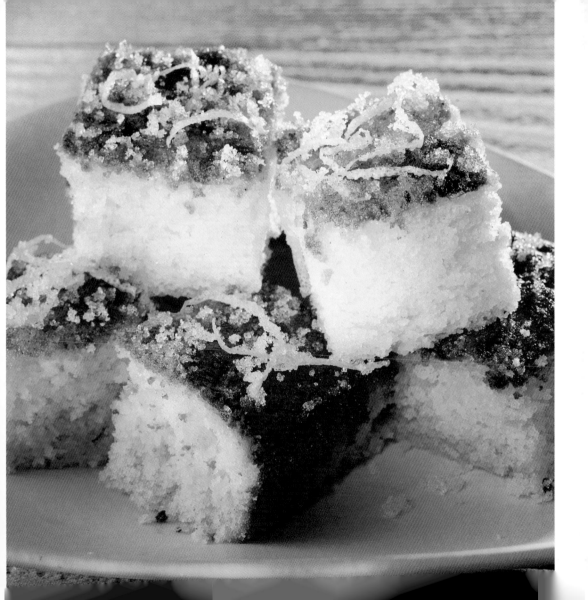

Carrot Cake

CUTS INTO 8–10

200 g/7 oz plain flour
½ tsp ground cinnamon
½ tsp freshly grated nutmeg
1 tsp baking powder
1 tsp bicarbonate of soda
150 g/5 oz dark
   muscovado sugar

200 ml/7 fl oz vegetable or
   sunflower oil
3 medium eggs
225 g/8 oz carrots, peeled
   and roughly grated
50 g/2 oz chopped walnuts

For the icing:
175 g/6 oz cream cheese
finely grated zest of 1 orange
1 tbsp orange juice
1 tsp vanilla extract
125 g/4 oz icing sugar

Preheat the oven to 150°C/300°F/Gas Mark 2, 10 minutes before baking. Lightly oil and line the base of a 15 cm/6 inch deep square cake tin with greaseproof paper or baking parchment.

Sift the flour, spices, baking powder and bicarbonate of soda together into a large bowl. Stir in the dark muscovado sugar and mix together.

Lightly whisk the oil and eggs together, then gradually stir into the flour and sugar mixture. Stir well. Add the carrots and walnuts. Mix thoroughly and then pour into the prepared cake tin. Bake in the preheated oven for 1¼ hours, or until light and springy to the touch and a skewer inserted into the centre of the cake comes out clean. Remove from the oven and allow to cool in the tin then turn out onto a wire rack. Leave until cold.

To make the icing, beat together the cream cheese, orange zest, orange juice and vanilla extract. Sift the icing sugar and stir into the cream cheese mixture.

When cold, discard the lining paper, spread the cream cheese icing over the top and serve cut into squares.

Store for 4–5 days, lightly covered in the refrigerator. I would not recommend freezing.

TASTY TIP

Ring the changes by replacing the nutmeg and ground cinnamon with 1 teaspoon of ground mixed spice. Also try adding 50 g/2 oz of raisins.

Easy Victoria Sponge

CUTS INTO 8–10

225 g/8 oz softened butter or
   margarine
225 g/8 oz caster sugar
4 medium eggs
1 tsp vanilla extract

225 g/8 oz self-raising flour
1 tsp baking powder
icing sugar, to dust

For the filling:
4 tbsp seedless
   raspberry jam
100 ml/3½ fl oz whipping
   cream (optional)

Preheat the oven to 180°C/350°F/Gas Mark 4. Grease two 20.5 cm/8 inch sandwich tins and line the bases with nonstick baking parchment.

Place the butter or margarine, sugar, eggs and vanilla extract in a large bowl and sift in the flour and baking powder. Beat for about 2 minutes until smooth and blended, and then divide between the tins and smooth level.

Bake for about 25 minutes until golden, well risen and the tops of the cakes spring back when lightly touched with a fingertip. Leave to cool in the tins for at least 5 minutes, then turn out onto a wire rack to cool. When cold, peel away the baking parchment.

When completely cold, spread one cake with jam and place on a serving plate. Whip the cream, if using, until it forms soft peaks, then spread on the underside of the other cake. Sandwich the two cakes together and sift a little icing sugar over the top.

Keep lightly covered in the refrigerator for 4–5 days.

If liked, the cake can be frozen in portions. Cut into portions and place on a plate. Freeze without wrapping, then, once solid, wrap in freezer wrap or kitchen foil. Label and date. Use within 2 weeks. When wishing to thaw, take out of the freezer and leave for 3–4 hours until soft.

Raspberry Butterfly Cupcakes

MAKES 6–7

50 g/2 oz caster sugar
50 g/2 oz softened butter or
  margarine
1 medium egg

50 g/2 oz self-raising flour
¼ tsp baking powder
½ tsp vanilla extract

To decorate:
2 tbsp seedless raspberry jam
6–7 fresh raspberries
icing sugar, to dust

Preheat the oven to 190°C/375°F/Gas Mark 5. Line a bun trays with 6–7 paper cases, depending on the depth of the holes.

Place all the cupcake ingredients in a large bowl and beat with an electric mixer or wooden spoon for about 2 minutes until smooth. Fill the paper cases halfway up with the mixture.

Bake for about 15 minutes until firm, risen and golden. Remove to a wire rack to cool. When cold, cut a small circle out of the top of each cupcake and then cut the circle in half to form wings.

Fill each cupcake with a teaspoon of raspberry jam. Replace the wings at an angle and top each with a fresh raspberry. Dust lightly with icing sugar and serve immediately.

If wishing to store, omit the fresh raspberries. Keep for up to 1 week in an airtight tin. It is not necessary to freeze.

TASTY TIP
For an extra treat,
fill the cut-out hollow
with freshly whipped
whipping cream.

Rice Pudding

MAKES 4 PORTIONS

65 g/2½ oz pudding rice
50 g/2 oz granulated sugar
410 g can evaporated milk

300 ml/½ pint
  semi-skimmed milk
pinch of freshly
  grated nutmeg

25 g/1 oz butter
jam, to decorate

Preheat the oven to 150°C/300°F/Gas Mark 2. Lightly oil a large ovenproof dish. Sprinkle the rice and the sugar into the dish and mix.

Bring the evaporated milk and milk to the boil in a small pan, stirring occasionally. Stir the milks into the rice and mix well until the rice is coated thoroughly. Sprinkle over the nutmeg, cover with kitchen foil and bake in the preheated oven for 30 minutes.

Remove the pudding from the oven and stir well, breaking up any lumps. Cover with the same kitchen foil. Bake in the preheated oven for a further 30 minutes. Remove from the oven and stir well again.

Dot the pudding with butter and bake for a further 45–60 minutes until the rice is tender and the skin is browned. Divide the pudding into 4 individual serving bowls. Top with a large spoonful of the jam and serve immediately.

Any remaining pudding can be spooned into a bowl, covered with clingfilm and kept in the refrigerator for up to 2 days. Do not freeze. To reheat, place the rice pudding into a small nonstick saucepan. Stir in sufficient milk so the pudding appears wet. Heat over a medium heat on the hob, stirring frequently with a wooden spoon until piping hot. The pudding can also be reheated in the microwave. Place in a bowl, cover with clingfilm and pierce 2–3 times. Heat on High for 2 minutes, leave to stand for 1 minute then stir and serve.

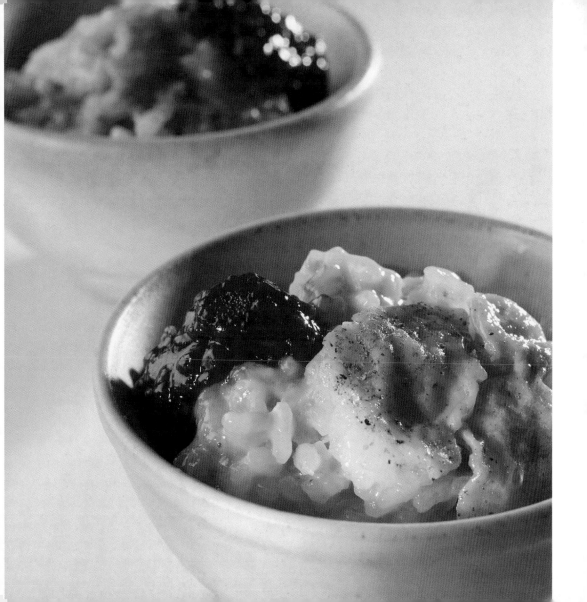

Poached Pears

MAKES 4 PORTIONS

2 small cinnamon sticks
125 g/4 oz caster sugar
300 ml/½ pint red wine or
blackcurrant juice

150 ml/¼ pint water
thinly pared zest and juice of
1 small orange
4 firm pears

orange slices, to decorate
vanilla yogurt, or ice cream,
to serve

Place the cinnamon sticks on the work surface and, with a rolling pin, slowly roll down the side of the cinnamon stick to bruise. Place in a large heavy-based saucepan.

Add the sugar, wine or blackcurrant juice, water, pared orange zest and juice to the pan and bring slowly to the boil, stirring occasionally, until the sugar is dissolved.

Meanwhile peel the pears, leaving the stalks on.

Cut out the cores from the bottom of the pears and level them so that they stand upright.

Stand the pears in the syrup, cover the pan and simmer for 20 minutes, or until tender.

Remove the pan from the heat and leave the pears to cool in the syrup, turning occasionally.

Arrange the pears on serving plates and spoon over the syrup. Decorate with the orange slices and serve with the yogurt or ice cream and any remaining juices.

Keep any remaining pears and juice in a bowl covered with clingfilm. Keep in the refrigerator for up to 1 week.

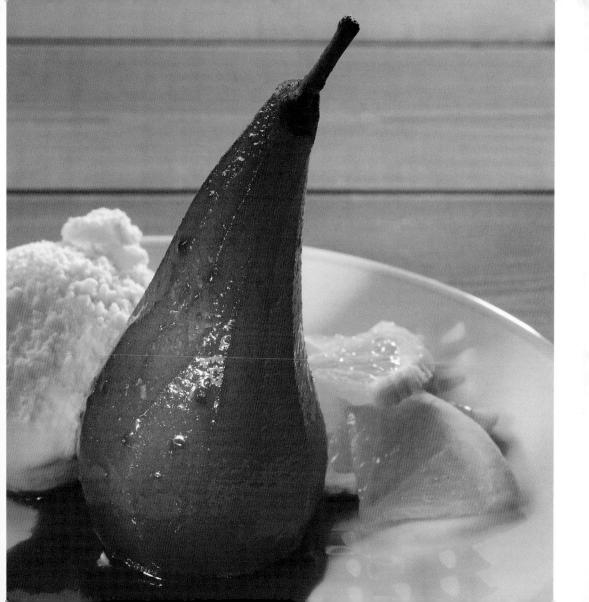

Chocolate & Fruit Crumble

MAKES 4 PORTIONS

For the crumble:
125 g/4 oz plain flour
125 g/4 oz softened butter
   or margarine
75 g/3 oz light soft
   brown sugar
50 g/2 oz rolled porridge oats
50 g/2 oz hazelnuts, chopped

For the filling:
450 g/1 lb Bramley apples
1 tbsp lemon juice
50 g/2 oz sultanas
50 g/2 oz seedless raisins
50 g/2 oz light soft
   brown sugar

350 g/12 oz pears, peeled,
   cored and chopped
1 tsp ground cinnamon
125 g/4 oz dark chocolate,
   very roughly chopped
2 tsp caster sugar
   for sprinkling

TASTY TIP

Bramley apples have a sharp
flavour and may need more
sugar than other apples. They
are ideal for cooking and
purée easily. If you prefer, use
a dessert apple like Golden
Delicious or Granny Smith.

Preheat the oven to 190°C/375°F/Gas Mark 5, 10 minutes before baking. Lightly oil an ovenproof dish. For the crumble, sift the flour into a large bowl. Cut the butter or margarine into small dice and add to the flour. Rub the butter or margarine into the flour until the mixture resembles fine breadcrumbs. Stir the sugar, porridge oats and chopped hazelnuts into the mixture and reserve.

For the filling, peel the apples, core and slice thickly. Place in a large heavy-based saucepan with the lemon juice and 3 tablespoons water. Add the sultanas, raisins and soft brown sugar. Bring slowly to the boil, cover and simmer over a gentle heat for 8–10 minutes, stirring occasionally, until the apples are slightly softened. Remove the saucepan from the heat and leave to cool slightly before stirring in the pears, ground cinnamon and the chopped chocolate. Spoon into the prepared ovenproof dish. Sprinkle the crumble evenly over the top then bake in the preheated oven for 35–40 minutes until the top is golden. Remove from the oven, sprinkle with the caster sugar and serve immediately.

Any remaining crumble can be spooned into a clean dish and covered with clingfilm. Keep overnight in the refrigerator. Do not freeze. The crumble will reheat well in the microwave. Pierce the clingfilm 2–3 times then heat on High for 2 minutes. Allow to stand for 1 minute then serve.

Chocolate Trifle

MAKES 4 PORTIONS

1½ bought chocolate
   Swiss rolls
4 tbsp strawberry jam
400 g can mangos or
   peaches, drained and
   juice reserved

200 g /7 oz fresh strawberries
200 g/7 oz dark chocolate
2 tbsp custard powder
2 tbsp granulated sugar
300 ml/½ pint
   semi-skimmed milk

300 ml/½ pint
   whipping cream
15 g/½ oz toasted
   flaked almonds

Slice the chocolate Swiss roll thickly and spread each slice with a little strawberry jam. Place the Swiss roll slices in the base of a trifle dish or glass bowl. Sprinkle over 4–5 tablespoons of reserved mango or peach juice and leave to stand for 10 minutes to let the juice soak into the Swiss roll. Slice the strawberries and dice the mango or peaches and reserve some for decoration. Scatter evenly over the Swiss roll with half the diced mango or peaches.

Break the chocolate into small pieces and place in a small heatproof bowl set over a saucepan of gently simmering water. Heat gently, stirring occasionally until the chocolate has melted and is smooth and free from lumps.

Blend the custard powder, sugar and milk to a smooth paste in a bowl, then pour into a heavy-based saucepan. Place over a gentle heat and cook, stirring constantly, until the custard is smooth and thick. Add the melted chocolate and stir until smooth and blended. Remove from the heat and leave to cool.

Spoon the custard mixture over the fruit and chill in the refrigerator for 1 hour. Whip the cream until soft peaks form and pile over the top of the set custard. Sprinkle over the toasted flaked almonds and decorate with the remaining strawberries and diced mango.

The trifle will keep for up to 3 days if kept in the refrigerator. Cover with clingfilm. Do not freeze.

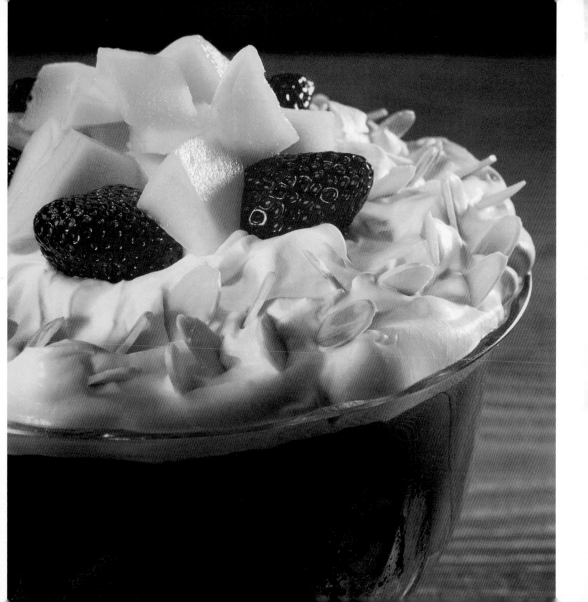

Chocolate Mousse with Raisins

MAKES 4 PORTIONS

200 g/7 oz dark chocolate
150 ml/¼ pint
   ready-made custard

300 ml/½ pint
   whipping cream
1 tbsp strong black coffee

125 g/4 oz raisins
1 medium egg white
chocolate curls, to decorate

Break the chocolate into small pieces and place in a small heatproof bowl set over a saucepan of gently simmering water. Heat gently, stirring occasionally, until the chocolate has melted and is smooth. Remove the bowl from the heat and leave to stand for about 10 minutes, or until the chocolate cools and begins to thicken. Using a metal spoon or rubber spatula, carefully fold in the prepared custard.

Whip the cream until soft peaks form, reserve a little for decorating and fold the rest into the chocolate custard mixture together with the coffee. Gently stir in the raisins.

Whisk the egg white in a clean, grease-free bowl, until stiff but not dry, then fold 1 tablespoon into the chocolate mixture and mix together lightly. Add the remaining egg white and stir lightly until well mixed. Spoon into 4 tall glasses and chill in the refrigerator for up to 2 hours.

Just before serving, top with whipped cream and decorate with the chocolate curls, then serve.

Keep any uneaten mousse in the refrigerator for up to 2 days. Do not freeze.

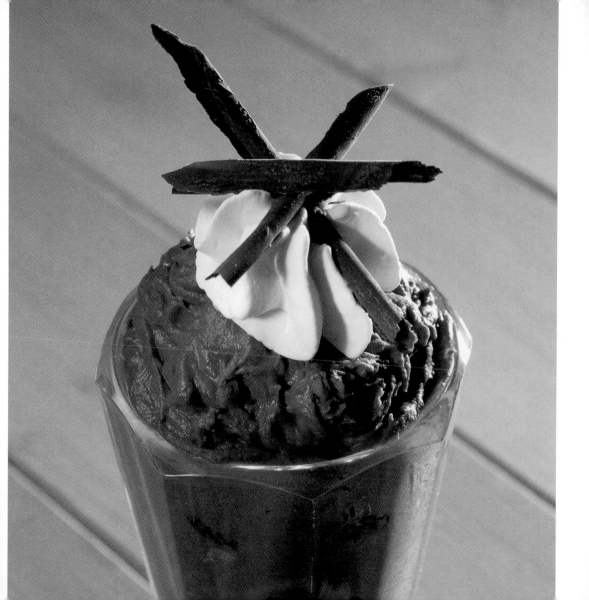

Chocolate Pancakes

MAKES 2 PORTIONS

For the pancakes:
40 g/1½ oz plain flour
2 tsp cocoa powder
1 tsp caster sugar
2 medium eggs
85 ml/3 fl oz milk
40 g/1½ oz unsalted
   butter, melted

For the mango sauce:
200 g/7 oz canned mango
   or 1 small ripe mango,
   peeled and diced
50 ml/2 fl oz clear apple
   juice or white wine
1 tbsp, or to taste, golden
   caster sugar

For the filling:
125 g/4 oz dark chocolate
50 ml/2 fl oz whipping cream
2 small eggs, separated
15 g/½ oz golden
   caster sugar

Preheat the oven to 200°C/400°F/Gas Mark 6, 15 minutes before cooking. Sift the flour, cocoa powder and sugar into a bowl and make a well in the centre. Beat the eggs and milk together, then gradually beat into the flour mixture to form a batter. Stir in 15 g/½ oz of the melted butter and leave to stand for 1 hour. Heat an 18 cm/7 inch frying pan and brush with a little melted butter. Add about 3 tablespoons of the batter and swirl to cover the base of the pan. Cook over a medium heat for 1–2 minutes, flip over and cook for a further 40 seconds. Repeat with the remaining batter. Stack the pancakes, interleaving with greaseproof paper.

To make the sauce, place the mango, apple juice or white wine and sugar in a saucepan and bring to the boil over a medium heat, then simmer for 2–3 minutes, stirring constantly. When it has thickened, chill in the refrigerator. For the filling, melt the chocolate and cream in a saucepan over a medium heat. Stir until smooth, then leave to cool. Beat the yolks with the caster sugar for 3–5 minutes until the mixture is pale and creamy, then beat in the chocolate mixture. Whisk the egg whites until stiff, and then add a little to the chocolate mixture. Stir in the remainder. Spoon a little of the mixture onto a pancake. Fold in half, then in half again. Repeat with the rest. Brush with butter and bake for 15–20 minutes until the filling is set. Serve hot or cold with the mango sauce. Uneaten pancakes can be refrigerated for up to 2 days, wrapped in clingfilm with the paper still separating them, or frozen in a freezer bag for up to 2 weeks. If frozen, allow the pancakes to thaw overnight. To reheat, lightly oil a frying pan and cook the pancakes for 1–2 minutes on both sides.

Fruited French Toast

MAKES 1–2 PORTIONS

2 slices spicy fruit loaf,
about 1 cm/½ inch thick
50 ml/2 fl oz milk
2 tbsp orange juice
1 medium egg yolk
¼ tsp, or to taste,
ground cinnamon

15 g/½ oz unsalted
butter
1 tbsp sunflower oil
2–3 tbsp seedless
raspberry jam
or conserve

For the orange cream:
125 ml/4 fl oz
whipping cream
1 tsp icing sugar
1 tbsp finely grated
orange zest
2 tsp orange juice

Cut the crusts off the bread, and then cut each slice diagonally into 4 triangles. Mix together half the milk and 1 tablespoon of the orange juice. Quickly dip the bread triangles in the mixture, and then place on a wire rack over a tray to drain.

Beat together the egg yolk, cinnamon, remaining milk and any milk on the tray. Dip the triangles in the egg and return to the rack.

Heat half the butter and the oil in a frying pan or wok. Add the bread triangles about 3 at a time and fry on both sides until well browned. Remove and keep warm in a low oven, while cooking the rest. When needed, add the remaining butter and finish cooking the bread triangles. Add to those keeping warm in the oven while making the sauce.

Gently heat the jam in a small saucepan with the remaining 1 tablespoon of orange juice and 1 tablespoon water until melted, and then cook for 1 minute.

To make the orange cream, whisk the cream, icing sugar, orange zest and orange juice together until soft peaks form. Serve the French toasts drizzled with the jam sauce and accompanied by the orange cream. These toasts will not keep, so it's a good excuse to invite a friend round to share.

HELPFUL HINT

The hot butter needs to be watched carefully in between batches. It may go brown, which will add a pleasant nutty flavour, but it is important to make sure that it does not burn.

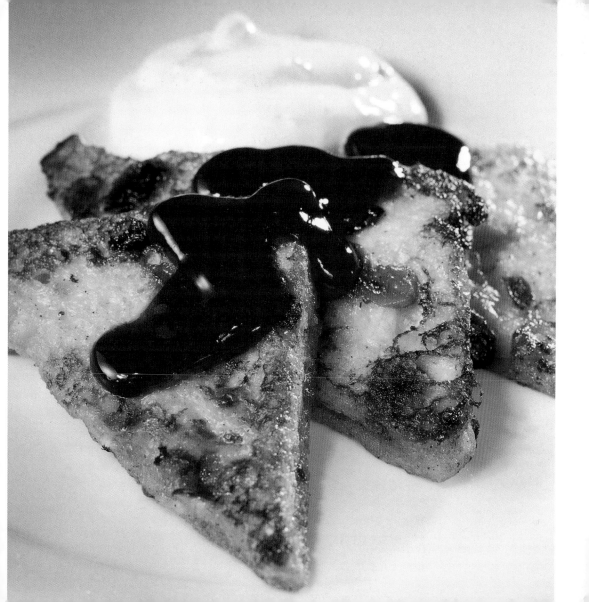

Index